WARTIME
LEICESTER

BEN BEAZLEY

First published in the United Kingdom in 2004 by
Sutton Publishing Limited · Phoenix Mill
Thrupp · Stroud · Gloucestershire · GL5 2BU

British Library Cataloguing in Publication Data
A catalogue record for this book is available from the British Library.

ISBN 0-7509-3671-1

Title page picture: Town Hall

Leicester ✦ Mercury

For my wife, Judith

Typeset in 11/12.5pt Sabon.
Typesetting and origination by
Sutton Publishing Limited.
Printed and bound in England by
J.H. Haynes & Co. Ltd, Sparkford.

Contents

Acknowledgements | 4

1. September 1939 | 5

2. Civil Defence | 23

3. The Phoney War: 1940 | 36

4. Bombing of Leicester | 51

5. Consolidation: 1941 | 70

6. The Middle Years: 1942–3 | 86

7. Rationing | 106

8. Planning Ahead: 1944 | 123

9. Women's Role | 138

10. The Final Months: 1945 | 152

11. Conclusion | 170

Appendices | 176

Glossary | 187

Bibliography | 188

Index | 189

Acknowledgements

This book could not have been written without the help of a number of people, all of whom I would like to take this opportunity to thank for their time and assistance, so freely given to me.

In particular, I would like to thank the following for their efforts on my behalf: the County Archivist, Carl Harrison, for allowing me access to the photographic library and archives at the Record Office for Leicestershire, Leicester and Rutland, and among his staff, Lois Edwards and Clive Chapman who have spent so much time tracing documents and other items on my behalf; the Editor of the *Leicester Mercury*, Nick Carter, for allowing me to reproduce the wealth of photographic material, without which this book would have been very lacking, along with Susan Hollins and Steve England of the *Mercury* staff, without whom achieving that task would not have been possible; Alan Jeffries of the Imperial War Museum, London, for supplying the answers to so many obscure queries; to Peter Condon who regularly produced new items of interest for me, David Simpson for his knowledge of military matters, Michael Ward for his numeracy skills, and Ian Coutts for ensuring that, despite my best efforts, my computer system never let me down – I am especially indebted.

I have to give a special thanks to Malcolm Tovey and John Warden for their encyclopedic knowledge of Leicester City Fire Service, and to the doyen of local history, Derek Seaton, for his help in City Council matters.

To all of those people, and to any others who I may inadvertently have missed, I extend my most grateful thanks.

Ben Beazley

CHAPTER ONE

September 1939

On the morning of Sunday 3 September 1939 the people of Leicester, along with the rest of the nation, tuned in their radios to hear what was to become one of the most momentous broadcasts in history.

At 11.15 a.m. Prime Minister Neville Chamberlain announced that 'this morning the British Ambassador in Berlin [Sir Nevile Meyrick Henderson] handed the German government a final note stating that unless we heard from them by eleven o'clock that they were prepared to at once withdraw their troops from Poland, a state of war would exist between us. I have to tell you now that no such undertaking has been received, and that consequently this country is at war with Germany.'

For the second time in twenty-one years the people of Britain were about to enter into a conflict of worldwide dimensions. On this occasion, however, they were far better prepared than they had been in 1914.

Since 1933, when Adolf Hitler became Chancellor of Germany, the progress of events within the Third Reich had been closely monitored by the British government. With the inevitability of another world war looming, as much as possible had been done – on the Home Front at least – to ensure a state of readiness.

One of the basic lessons learned from the First World War was that the key to defeating an enemy lay in the disruption of its economy. If that objective could be secured, the ensuing inability to maintain a war industry and the consequent demoralisation of its people would follow. Technological advances during the 1920s and '30s – especially in the field of aviation – made this objective eminently achievable. There was a general appreciation that, for the first time, any future war could now depend as much on the protection and security of the Home Front, as on what took place on the battlefield.

Within a short space of time after 1933 Hitler's militaristic ambitions, along with the consequences for Europe, became obvious. From as early as 1935, both at national and local level, steps were being taken to ensure the safety of Britain's civilian population.

Under the title Civil Defence, the creation of a series of wartime emergency services was undertaken across the country. In September 1935 a circular was issued to local authorities giving advice and recommendations on air-raid precautions. By 1937 these recommendations had become mandatory, and in April of that year the Air Raid Wardens Service was created.

The primary role of the ARP, as it became known, was to establish Warden's Posts and control centres in towns and cities from which, in the case of aerial attack, rescue and recovery work would be coordinated. It was only as time progressed that the image of the man in a dark boiler suit and tin hat patrolling the streets in the dead of night and exhorting householders to 'put that light out!' took hold. The official definition of a warden was – and remained throughout the war – 'that he should be a responsible member of the public, chosen to be a leader and

A city centre newspaper seller, September 1939. *(Courtesy of* Leicester Mercury*)*

Taken in June 1938, this *Leicester Evening Mail* photograph shows the Minister for Air Raid Precautions, Geoffrey Lloyd, inspecting a squad of volunteers in gas protection suits at the British United Shoe Machinery Co. *(Courtesy of Leicestershire Records Office)*

advisor of his neighbours in a small area – a street or group of streets – in which he is known and respected'.

The provisions for Civil Defence were to encompass everything, from recruiting extra men as volunteers into the Fire and Police Services to the establishment of the Police Auxiliary Messenger Service and the Women's Voluntary Service. Householders were to be supplied with air-raid shelters for their gardens, and plans were laid to construct public shelters in populated areas. First-Aid Posts, manned by the casualty services – ambulance workers and St John Ambulance volunteers – were to be set up in designated buildings such as church halls and schoolrooms.

The authority primarily responsible for ensuring the safety of the citizens of Leicester was the City Council. In line with the government's guidelines its elected members had been carefully making provisions for the fateful day over a long period of time. Two of the people responsible for the implementation of any plans were the Chief Officer of the City Fire Brigade, Francis Winteringham, and the Chief Constable, Oswald Cole.

Not unexpectedly, their areas of responsibility ran closely together and required them to coordinate their activities from an early stage. Francis Winteringham, who had only come to Leicester as Head of the Fire Brigade in June 1938, was appointed

Members of the public participate with Civil Defence volunteers in a First-Aid exercise. Note the new uniforms worn by the ARP Wardens and the distinctive 'W' on the steel helmets. *(Courtesy of Leicestershire Records Office)*

ARP Controller. It was obvious that his main area of expertise was going to be in relation to the damage caused by fires to buildings in the city and the subsequent removal of casualties. (Until August 1940, the Leicester City Fire Brigade was responsible for providing an ambulance service for the city.)

Oswald John Buxton Cole, who had been Chief Constable of the city since January 1929, undertook the recruiting and training of Air Raid Wardens. In preparation for this role, in the summer of 1936 Inspector Harold Poole and Sergeant Walter Broadhurst of the City Police were sent off to the new Home Office Air Raid Precautions Anti-Gas Training Centre at Falfield in Gloucestershire. Volunteers for the new Warden Service were in ready supply and by June 1938 a large number of men were trained and held in readiness.

During the months immediately prior to war being declared both Winteringham and Cole were also fully engaged in recruiting volunteers into support units for their respective organisations.

The Air Raid Precautions Act of 1937 gave Chief Fire Officers the opportunity to draft into their ranks volunteer fire-fighters, and by early 1938 men and women were being inducted nationally into the Auxiliary Fire Service (AFS) for attachment to local brigades. By mid-July 1939 Winteringham was in a position to announce that his brigade was coming to a state of readiness. Granby Halls, originally built as a training centre in the latter part of the First World War, had been acquired for use by the AFS, and eighteen trailer pumps together with thirty-six hydraulic jacks and a thousand respirators for fire-fighters had been delivered to Brigade Headquarters in Lancaster Place. Although in the early days recruiting into the AFS was not producing

Between 1938 and 1939, while the country was preparing for war, everyone in the workplace, both male and female, was encouraged to become involved in air-raid and gas training. This young lady is part of the staff working at the John Bull factory. *(Courtesy of Leicestershire Records Office)*

Taking part in an exercise, early on in the war, police and volunteers man the Civil Defence Control Room. The figure seated on the left in the foreground is Police Sergeant (later Deputy Chief Constable) Bernard Ecob. *(Courtesy of Leicestershire Records Office)*

the results that Winteringham had envisaged, his request for permission to purchase five hundred uniforms indicates the number of volunteers he had targeted.

Arrangements for the supplementing of police forces nationally were somewhat more diverse and – with hindsight – unnecessarily complicated.

In 1920, in the aftermath of the First World War, the Home Office drew up a set of guidelines for the formation of a First Police Reserve, made up of retired regular police officers, which could be mobilised should a state of emergency be declared. These men were to receive a retainer of £3 annually, and on mobilisation would be paid weekly at the lowest rate applicable to the rank which they held on retirement. Under these arrangements a unit of eighteen retired City Police officers had been in place since May 1936. (In 1938 there were twenty-eight men in this unit of which only two remained at the end of the war.)

A Police War Reserve, formed initially to serve only in the Metropolitan and City of London Forces, was quickly extended to the provinces. This Reserve, made up of men who were engaged as full-time Constables, was intended to fill the gaps created by regular officers being called up into His Majesty's Forces. In 1940 a Police War Reserve establishment of 187 officers was created in Leicester city. Always maintained as a small unit, the highest number of men serving in this Reserve during the war was 122 in 1941.

With the outbreak of war in September 1939, a huge national recruiting campaign was launched to fill the ranks of the Auxiliary Fire Service.

Members of the ARP Committee inspecting an air-raid shelter in Belgrave Gate, 2 September 1939. From left to right: Cllr Chas Keene (Chair, ARP Comm.), Arthur Gooseman (City Surveyor), F.G. Bailey (Clerk to ARP Comm.), Francis Winteringham (Chief Officer, Leics City Fire Brigade), Thos Wilkie (Lighting Engineer), Cllr Chas Gillot (ARP Comm.). *(Courtesy of Leicestershire Records Office, D. Seaton and J. Collinson)*

Strenuous efforts were made during the pre-war years to recruit men into the Special Constabulary. After 1918 the establishment of Special Constables had been allowed to deteriorate dramatically and by the 1930s, of those Constables still shown in its ranks, a large number were over sixty years of age. At the end of April 1939 a recruiting drive under the direction of Deputy Chief Constable John Gabbitas resulted in 314 men being recruited.

At a very early stage in the war, with a view to filling gaps in general service areas, a Women's Auxiliary Police Corps was established. Although their remit was quite a wide one – clerical, telephone and domestic work along with driving and maintaining motor vehicles – Cole does not appear to have taken particular advantage of the scheme. Having engaged fourteen women to work as telephonists in May 1940, he thereafter allowed the number to fall until in 1945 there were only two.

During this period one aspect of security which was of special concern to Chief Constables was the mainland activities of the Irish Republican Army. In 1939 the IRA was extremely active in cities throughout Great Britain, including Leicester. In an estimated 130 bomb attacks up and down the country (of which 60 were in London), several people were killed and a large amount of property damaged.

In Leicester, soon after seven o'clock on the evening of Saturday 2 July 1939, a dark-haired man in his middle twenties got off a train from Birmingham at the LMS railway station in London Road and asked the ticket collector to look after his suitcase while he 'nipped out'. When the collector's relief, Charles Venn, took over at ten o'clock that night the man had not returned for his case which was still in the attendant's cabin. As it was holiday time the station was busy throughout the night with excursion trains returning from the coast. Around twenty minutes to four in the morning, Venn was chatting with a man who was waiting for his wife to arrive on an excursion train from Brighton when they became aware of a hissing sound and the acrid smell of a fuse burning. Realising that there was a bomb in the collector's cabin, both men ran into the booking hall seconds before the explosion. Although neither of them was seriously injured (Charles Venn received numerous cuts from flying glass), extensive damage was caused to the station concourse. Only a short time earlier a crowd of schoolchildren returning from a day trip had passed through the area where the explosion occurred.

On 29 August, in what was presumed to be another IRA attempt to disrupt communications in the city, the wires to a dozen telephone kiosks were cut. With an isolated box being sabotaged on the A47 out of Leicester, it was assumed that those responsible were passing through the town in a vehicle.

Councillor Charles Keene was one of the leading figures in ensuring that Leicester was ready for the exigencies of war. Among other things, from September 1939 until July 1941 he served as ARP Controller for the city before handing over the role to Charles Worthington. (Courtesy of Leicestershire Records Office)

Workmen digging out a public air-raid shelter on Imperial Avenue near to the school. Note in the background the white 'blackout' markings painted along the kerb edges. *(Courtesy of Leicestershire Records Office)*

Unlike the prelude to the First World War, when Emmeline Pankhurst's Suffragettes had called a halt to their programme of sabotage, the IRA was to continue its activities throughout the forthcoming years.

The City Council, for its part, set about creating an administrative system which would enable the complex network of provisions being implemented in Leicester to function efficiently. An ARP Committee and an Emergency Committee, both under the Chairmanship of Councillor Charles Keene were initiated. The members of these two committees were given very wide powers to expedite matters in the city and by the end of the first year, on more than one occasion, received censure for the autocracy which they were displaying.

On 5 September, two days after war was declared, in anticipation of food rationing being imposed and in line with government policy, a Food Control Committee for the city was introduced.

At the head of the commission was the Town Clerk, Lawrence McEvoy, assisted by his deputy John Finlinson, who was to be responsible for the issue of ration books. The remainder of the group was made up of the Deputy Lord Mayor, Councillor Frank Acton, and representatives of local trade in the city. In addition to

Members of the Auxiliary Territorial Service in training at Strensall camp, near York in July 1939. Here they are being instructed in the use of a 3-inch mortar by soldiers of the King's Own Yorkshire Light Infantry. *(Courtesy of* Leicester Mercury*)*

Staff of a local factory in the city being shown how to put on their gasmasks. *(Courtesy of Leicestershire Records Office)*

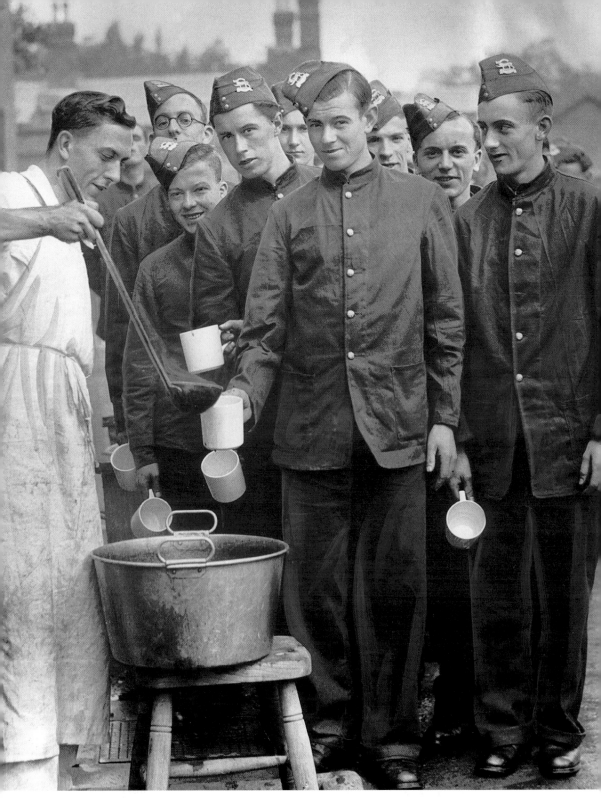

Militia men at Glen Parva depot, July 1939. Conscription was introduced in April 1939. Men were allowed to choose which branch of the Services they wanted to go into – British Army, Royal Navy or Royal Air Force. Those who chose the Army were initially drafted into what was known as 'the Militia'. *(Courtesy of* Leicester Mercury*)*

provisions being made in respect of food it was seen as inevitable that petrol rationing would follow within a very short time.

Viewed from the perspective of the average man and woman in Leicester, the year 1939 prior to September had been in many ways an eventful one. While having to continue with their normal everyday lives people were acutely aware, during the latter months, that a war with Germany was virtually inevitable – it was more a question of 'when' rather than 'if'.

The years since the previous war, which the nation had been promised was 'the war to end all wars', had not been easy. Following the General Strike in 1926 unemployment and the Depression of the 1930s had coloured almost everyone's life. Unlike August 1914 when men had flocked to the Colours for a short engagement and the adventure of a lifetime, people now understood very clearly the realities of what another war held for them. Memories were still fresh in everyone's minds of losses and bereavements in every street. The phrase 'back by Christmas' had long since been replaced by Kipling's more sobering lines, 'if any should ask why we died, Tell them because our fathers lied'.

Leicester, with a population of around 240,000 people (the 1931 Census showed a total of 239,169 inhabitants in the city), was, in spite of the depressed years of the '30s, still a reasonably prosperous city. The main daily newspaper – the *Leicester Mercury* – cost 1*d*; a packet of cigarettes was on average 6*d* for ten or 11½*d* for twenty. A man could still buy a decent sports coat from Lewis' for 21*s*, a suit for 37*s* 6*d*, and a raincoat for a guinea. Ladies seeking a new summer outfit could expect to pay 10*s* 6*d* for a frock, 30*s* for a coat, and most expensive of all, 3*s* 11*d* for a pair of stockings. Semi-detached houses being built by Webster and Finn of Harrison Road, on the 'New Stadium estate' cost a maximum of £550, while a rented house on the Stocking Farm estate was priced at 14*s* 8*d* a week including rates and water charges.

Until the end of August, despite a not particularly good summer, both rail and coach companies continued to advertise 'the charm of late August and September holidays'. For 11*s* 6*d* an adult could take a day trip on the bus to London, or book a return fare to the east coast for 21*s* 6*d*.

Following Hitler's occupation first of the Sudetenland and then Czechoslovakia, war became inevitable and the summer of 1939 saw frantic activity on the military front. On 1 July Army Reservists were served with call-up papers. Thirty-four thousand men across the country each received a postal order for 4*s* (which they were told would be deducted from their army pay), and a railway voucher with instructions as to which depot they should report. Notice was given that RAF Reservists were to be called up as part of a training exercise. Ships of the Royal Navy were put on standby for fleet exercises and 70,000 Reservists (including 12,000 officers) were recalled.

Advertisements appeared in local papers for volunteers aged eighteen to thirty-two to join the Royal Air Force Reserve as wireless operators and air gunners.

On 1 July crowds of Leicester people were treated to a military display in Victoria Park by the newly formed 2/5th Battalion of the Leicestershire Regiment under the command of Lt Col Guy German. (Constituted under the 'doubling' of the Territorial Army, and based at Eastern Boulevard, this was the unit's first public appearance. In 1940, as Commanding Officer of the 1/5th Battalion, Guy German became a prisoner of war during the Norway Campaign.) At the end of the month several hundred of these same citizens lined up to watch as the battalion marched off to entrain for the

Territorial Army's annual camp at Holyhead. Departing the same morning for the training camp was the 1/5th Battalion commanded by Lt Col J.C. Barrett VC.

The women of the 1st Company Auxiliary Territorial Service (ATS) – which had originally been formed in 1934 as the Voluntary Emergency Service – set off on 11 July from the Great Central railway station for a fifteen-day camp at Strensall in Yorkshire. On 12 August 600 men of the 115th Field Regiment Royal Artillery (formerly the 239th Battery) departed from the city for camp at Bridlington.

July and August also saw the skies over England and France busy with a series of combined flying exercises between the air forces of the two countries. Throughout the morning of 25 July two hundred Wellington and Blenheim bombers of the RAF flew over the English Channel to Paris, Lyons and the Bay of Biscay in a simulated air attack.

While this first operation passed off without event, a second during the August bank holiday was a disaster. Despite very bad weather conditions a decision was taken by the RAF to run a three-day exercise involving 1,300 aircraft. During the early hours of Tuesday 8 August the crew of a Wellington was lost in the North Sea, 17 miles off the coast of Yarmouth. In two other accidents four men were killed when a bomber crashed at Tollerton in Yorkshire, and the crew of another Wellington bailed out when the aircraft got into difficulties over Thetford in Norfolk. On this occasion the pilot managed to land the plane in nearby woodland.

In a slightly bizarre incident the same weekend an aircraft on a local training flight over the county got into difficulties and, apparently trying to crash land in Victoria Park, came down on the outskirts of Leicester. Piloted by twenty-year-old Cadet Frederick Rooney from Coventry, the aircraft went out of control over the city and, narrowly missing an ice-cream salesman on his 'stop me and buy one' tricycle, crashed in University Road, bursting into flames. Firemen, who had watched the incident from the nearby Brigade Headquarters in Lancaster Place, attended the scene and rescued the young man from the blazing aeroplane. Although the area was closed off for some time while the debris was cleared no one other than the pilot – who suffered severe lacerations – was injured.

After the famous Sunday morning broadcast by Chamberlain announcing that Britain was at war with Germany, world events began to move quickly. At 2 p.m. that afternoon Australia, followed by New Zealand, proclaimed a state of war. A few hours later France joined the Allies, and Canada gave an assurance of effective cooperation. During the evening the Prime Minister established a War Cabinet which included as First Lord of the Admiralty, Britain's future war leader, Winston Churchill.

On 6 September President Franklin Delano Roosevelt on behalf of the American people signed a proclamation declaring the United States to be a neutral country. The document, which was to effectively keep America out of the war until December 1941, laid down among other things that no US national should enlist as a soldier or sailor in any of the belligerents' armed forces.

On 2 September 1939, as a preparatory measure, the British government introduced compulsory military service for all men between eighteen and forty-one years of age. This was followed on 29 September by 'National Registration Day', when all householders were required to fill in and submit registration papers prior to being issued with identity cards which, for the duration of the war, had to be carried with them at all times.

Petrol rationing which was brought into force before the end of September would, the City Council warned, result in reduced bus services in those districts of the city which were also served by the tramways.

From a military standpoint Britain in 1939 was not in a strong position. In the years between the wars the strength of the army had been run down from 3½ million men to 370,000. Equally as important, the ability of the nation's manufacturing industry to supply munitions had also been allowed to deteriorate. Despite efforts to double the size of the Territorial Army since March 1939, when the British Expeditionary Force set off for France on 11 September it comprised only four divisions with 158,000 men.

At the end of 1918 Britain had an air force of 3,300 first-line aircraft; five years later this number had been reduced to 371. Although plans were put into place during the 1920s to remedy this situation it was not until after 1933, when the potential of a German arms build-up was fully realised, that an RAF Expansion Plan was implemented. In an early example of Britain's dependency on supplies from an as yet neutral America, it was announced at the beginning of July 1939 that the first of the giant bomber flying boats (Catalinas), built for the RAF in San Diego, United States, were to be flown across the Atlantic to England via Botwood, Newfoundland.

The country's main strength lay in the Royal Navy, which at the outbreak of war was the strongest in the world. Before mobilisation it numbered 9,762 officers and 109,170 ratings. In January 1939, in addition to those already serving, there were 51,485 men in the Royal Fleet Reserve, 6,180 in the Royal Naval Volunteer Reserve and 10,038 merchant seamen in the Royal Naval Reserve.

While the British Expeditionary Force under Gen Lord Gort VC embarked for France, it was initially the RAF and the Royal Navy who took the fight to the enemy.

On 3 September an RAF Blenheim of 139 Squadron (Wyton) flew over the German naval base at Wilhelmshaven taking aerial photographs. As a result of the information gained from this reconnaissance, a bombing raid the following day in very bad weather scored several direct hits on enemy vessels in the Schilling Roads and Kiel Canal.

In recognition of this raid the first gallantry decorations of the war were conferred on two of the pilots involved, both of whom received the Distinguished Flying Cross. The first of these was awarded to Flg Off Andrew MacPherson for his part in the photographic mission. The second was to an ex-Leicester man, 26-year-old Flg Off Kenneth Christopher Doran, who until 1924 had lived with his parents at 23 Thurlow Road in Clarendon Park.

The *Gazette* entry for Flg Off Doran states that: 'Early in September this officer led an attack against an enemy cruiser in the face of heavy anti-aircraft fire, and under extremely bad weather conditions he pressed home a successful low level attack with great determination.' The *Leicester Mercury* report of 11 October is a little more specific, declaring that 'single handed [Doran] attacked a German pocket battleship at Wilhelmshaven, one of the Naval bases in the North Sea, near to the entrance to the Kiel Canal. He had to face the full fury of the cruiser's anti-aircraft guns, yet managed to score several direct hits with his bombs.'

While from a military standpoint the latter months of 1939 lapsed into what became known as the 'phoney war', on the Home Front measures to ensure the safety of the civilian population were progressing vigorously.

Between 1 and 4 September mass evacuation plans to move several thousand children and hospital patients out of cities thought to be at risk from aerial bombardment were put into operation. With the country divided up into 'evacuation', 'neutral', and 'reception areas', the programme was from the outset ambitious. The plans had been in place for some time and on 31 August, three days prior to Neville Chamberlain's broadcast to the nation, the following evacuation estimates for the movement of children were made public:

From London:		
154,000	to	Kent
151,000	to	East Sussex
124,000	to	Essex
95,000	to	Surrey
84,000	to	Hertford
83,000	to	West Sussex
2,400	to	Rutland

From Liverpool and Merseyside:	216,000 to	Wales

From Manchester:	247,000 to	Lancashire, Shropshire, Staffordshire

In Leicestershire notice was given that Hinckley district would receive 5,000 women and children (Earl Shilton, Barwell, Burbage and Stoke Goulding would take only children). The county was designated to accept 12,000 children from the Sheffield district, of which between 1,400 and 3,500 would be accommodated in the Melton Mowbray area. (Figures are not shown for Leicester itself, and it is probable that as a city it was considered to be a neutral area which could be at risk of attack.)

In the event the scheme, while well intentioned, was not a resounding success. Certainly in the Leicestershire area the actual numbers of children evacuated into the county does not seem to bear any relationship to the government's projections. Figures published on 1 October show that Ashby-de-la-Zouch received 625 children, Ibstock 400, Barlestone 100, Market Bosworth 60, Ravenstone 40, and Hinckley 550.

One reason for this shortfall in the government's estimates could well be that initially the numbers were inflated on the basis that it was safer to overestimate. What is more likely is that at the point when it was announced that the scheme was to be implemented, many parents refused to be parted from their children, choosing to keep them at home. Although provision had been made by the County Council for 30,000 children to be moved into Leicestershire, at the end of the month only a third – 10,000 – had in fact arrived. Probably the most disappointing – and disturbing – factor was the number of children who within a matter of weeks were removed from the fostering environment and taken home by their parents. The reasons for this are quite clear.

The evacuation programme was conducted with little consideration for the welfare of either the children involved or the families who were going to foster them.

When those who were to be evacuated arrived at the railway stations from which they were to depart, they were put arbitrarily on to the first available train. In this manner siblings, school friends and neighbours were split up and sent to different parts of the country, ensuring that many of the children arrived at their destination totally isolated.

Nor was any consideration given to matching the social backgrounds of the evacuees to those with whom they were going to live. The result was that on many occasions children from an extremely poor inner city background were placed with middle- to upper-class families, resulting in an intensely unhappy situation for all concerned.

Neither was a ready supply of volunteers to take in evacuees particularly forthcoming. Local authorities were often obliged to place notices in newspapers warning that where there was a dearth of households offering to participate in the scheme, then billeting orders would be made.

A major area of discontent was the standard allowance paid to those with whom evacuees were living – 10s 6d was paid per week for the first child and 8s 6d for each subsequent child. In a household where the evacuated mother was billeted along with her children, the occupant had a responsibility only to provide adequate lodgings and consequently received on a weekly basis 5s for the mother and 3s for each child. In this situation the children's mother was expected to buy and cook her family's food out of her own money.

Within a very short period of time the children began to flood back to the cities whence they had come. The Clerk to the Leicestershire County Council, L.E. Rumsey, reported on 31 October – less than eight weeks into the programme – that of those children accommodated in the county at:

Barrow on Soar	out of 1,300 children	700 had returned home
Hinckley	" " 1,916 children	893 " " "
Market Harborough	" " 1,590 children	400 " " "
Lutterworth	" " 200 children	8 " " "
Melton Mowbray	" " 583 children	328 " " "
Shepshed	" " 236 children	82 " " "

Significantly, a common complaint related to the money spent by foster parents on the children from poor families, who had now decamped taking with them clothing and shoes which had been bought for them.

The problem was not peculiar to the Leicestershire district. In Birmingham out of 4,135 mothers and 7,858 children under five years of age, 90 per cent had returned home within a very short period.

As in August 1914, following a brief moment of uncertainty, the manufacturing industries in the city picked up and by December unemployment figures for the city and county were 4,000 less than for the same period in the previous year. The boot and shoe trades in particular, along with hosiery and engineering, recovered rapidly.

The situation almost exactly mirrored that which existed in Leicester during the first months of the previous war. Munitions for war were classed as anything from armaments and shells to socks and underclothes for HM Forces. Leicester, as a prosperous industrial town situated at the hub of a main railway system in the centre of the country, was well placed to provide those munitions.

The building trade on the other hand, and to an extent some service industries, suffered initially because of the war. As a consequence of the government ordering a halt to local authority capital works, and a cessation of the building of new houses, many construction workers suddenly found themselves on short time. In October Leicester Electricity Department laid off 200 casual staff. The Chief Engineer and Manager of the department, John Mould, pointed out regretfully that pre-war his men were installing as many as 500 services a week – this figure was now down to around 40.

In his first budget speech of the war the Chancellor of the Exchequer, Sir John Simon, announced an increase of 2s in income tax, raising it from 5s to 7s 6d. Whisky jumped from 12s 6d a bottle to 13s 9d, beer went up by 1d a pint and tobacco by 3d an ounce. Of particular relevance to the housewife, the price of sugar was increased by 1d a pound.

As November 1939 approached the City Council settled down to decide how much money they should pay to Corporation employees (including police and firemen), who were away on active service, in order to make up their army allowances. This was a problem which beset local authorities over the entire country. During the First World War all such employees had been treated as being temporarily away from their place of employment and their wages had been made up in full. The resulting budgetary implications over a period of four years had been disastrous and were not about to be repeated. The decision eventually reached by Leicester City Council was that each man should be paid only a percentage of his wage. A corollary to the absence of Corporation workers was the likelihood that, for the first time in two decades, the employment of female conductors on buses and tram cars would have to be once more considered.

After nearly four months of uncertainty and intense activity – compounded by the prospect of one of the hardest winters in living memory – in common with every other town in England, Leicester settled down to await the outcome of what promised to be a long war.

CHAPTER TWO

Civil Defence

D uring the weeks prior to September 1939 preparations had been made in both the city and the county to put into place an effective system of air-raid precautions.

In July Lord Cromwell was appointed Chief Air Raid Warden for Leicestershire, with Lord Trent as Regional Commissioner, and the county divided up into six separate districts: Ashby, Leicester North, Market Harborough, Hinckley, Melton Mowbray and Loughborough.

In the city under the Chairmanship of Charles Keene, assisted by John Frears and Charles Gillot, a small ARP Committee (soon to become known as 'the Committee of Three') was formed and made responsible for organising the measures necessary for the protection of Leicester and its environs.

As the organisations responsible for the main emergency services, both the Fire Brigade and the City Police Force set about the task of making their respective headquarters safe. At Charles Street Police Station steps were taken to make the building gas and bomb proof, and shower facilities were built for men coming off duty who had been in contact with poison gas. Protective clothing and respirators were stored, while steel shuttering (at a cost of £2,000) was put up at the windows. Over 80,000 bags of sand, reaching up to the first-floor level, were stacked against the outer walls of the police station by off duty police officers as a protection against blast damage. The bags, when finally in place, contained 800 tons of sand – purchased locally from a builder for £118. Unfortunately, fourteen months later in December 1940 they had to be removed at a cost of £130, as the weight had caused the pavements beneath to collapse and sink.

An auxiliary control room manned by the police was installed in the basement of the town hall, and the top floor of the Newarke Girls School on Imperial Avenue was equipped with a fifty-line telephone switchboard to be used as a back-up should the one at the main police station be knocked out.

Similarly, at Fire Brigade Headquarters, showers were restructured and converted into air-raid shelters for firemen on standby. Extra tie lines were installed between the Brigade control room, the town hall and each of the seven ARP reporting centres.

While a small army of Air Raid Wardens was being recruited and trained by the police, notices informing the public what to do in the case of attack began to appear all over the town in the week prior to 3 September. Stocks of protective clothing, respirators and bleach were delivered and put into Corporation stores. Over 2 million bags of sand for the protection of public buildings were made ready for distribution. In streets all around the city signs began to appear directing citizens to the nearest public air-raid shelters.

Orders were given that all the lights in the Clock Tower area must be switched off, and cinemas and shops were instructed to extinguish their exterior lighting.

As part of the 'gas awareness' campaigns organised by the authorities, large groups of people took part in exercises designed to simulate large-scale gas attacks. *(Courtesy of Leicestershire Records Office)*

Sand, stored on the traffic island opposite Charles Street Police Station, was put into bags and stacked against the walls of the station to protect it against bomb blast. Here, off-duty policemen, assisted by a gang of small boys, are engaged in the task during the late summer of 1939. Unfortunately, owing to the weight of the sandbags, the pavements around the police station collapsed just over a year later and the sandbags had to be removed. *(Courtesy of Leicestershire Records Office)*

Notices were posted declaring that if enemy aircraft were sighted, 'the warning signal [siren] is a warbling note sounded for two minutes. The all-clear is one continuous note. If there is a danger of a gas attack Wardens will sound rattles. The all-clear from a gas attack will be signalled by the ringing of hand bells.'

At the beginning of the weekend of 25 August all City Police leave was cancelled and Police War Reservists called up for duty. At the same time each of the Corporation departments with a responsibility for the supply and distribution of ARP stores was manned around the clock, and fifty men were sent to the depot in Erskine Street to begin assembling the stockpile of one thousand gasmasks held there. Gangs of workmen began to dig trenches for the construction of shelters in Town Hall Square near to the temporary war memorial.

On the outskirts of the town Roecliffe Manor, which served as an auxiliary hospital to the Leicester Royal Infirmary, was evacuated in readiness for use as a casualty centre, as was the Overstrand Convalescent Home which was administered by the Saturday Hospital Society.

In anticipation of imminent enemy action, Corporation employees were deployed all over the city to mask traffic lights and black out bollards. The control board at the Street Lighting Department, for the time being – with all street lights turned off – redundant, was reassigned to be used by the ARP Committee for the management of shelter lighting and other emergency services.

Initially the total discontinuance of street lighting (around 45 per cent of the city streets still had gas lamps) led to the lighting depots at Western Road, Asfordby Street, Bulwer Road in Clarendon Park, and Melrose Street being closed down and the staff, who were employed as lamplighters, laid off. As many as possible of these men were temporarily reassigned to ARP duties.

Once it was appreciated that plunging the city into total darkness by turning out all of the street lamps was impractical, the engineers at the Lighting Department began to explore other options, and during 1940 came up with a system of reduced level illumination known as 'star lighting'. Invisible to aircraft flying overhead, the new system was installed in (an estimated) 50 per cent of the town's streets, and alleviated considerably the problems encountered by pedestrians and vehicular traffic. (Accidents, some of them fatal, became a common occurrence during the blackout with people stepping out in front of vehicles – often tram cars or buses – that were running with hardly any lights.)

On 1 September Francis Winteringham, the Chief Officer of the Leicester City Fire Brigade, was provided with offices at 24 Halford Street, designated ARP Controller and given day-to-day control of all ARP work. One of Winteringham's first moves as Controller was to call up a small number (about 20 per cent) of those who had volunteered to be full-time Air Raid Wardens and First Aiders. A prime consideration for such a conservative number of people was that a degree of controversy had sprung up concerning the wages paid to full-time Civil Defence workers. For working a twelve-hour shift, seven days a week, a full-time male warden received approximately £3 a week and a female £2. Many others who gave their services voluntarily – albeit part time – without such remuneration felt that this was unfair. At the same time elements of the City Council were also loath to spend money in this manner.

Members of groups 4 and 5, 'G' Div. ARP, returning from church parade in November 1940. Uniform for the ARP was at this stage still being standardised, as is evident by the mixture of tunics and boiler suits. Some carry a mackintosh, one at the front of the nearest column has a winter greatcoat, while the lady at the rear of the same line is in civilian clothing. Initially, the uniform comprised a set of blue overalls and a silver badge. By May 1941 almost all units were equipped with blue serge uniforms and a beret. *(Courtesy of* Leicester Mercury)

Winteringham subsequently took out an advertisement in the *Leicester Mercury* for badly needed volunteers to make up the numbers that he was short of in the various Civil Defence branches:

Auxiliary Fire Service	men over 25
Fire Brigade Reserve	men over 25 with Fire Brigade experience
Air Raid Wardens	men over 30
First Aid Parties	men over 30
First Aid Post Staff	men over 30 and women
Rescue Parties	men over 25 who are building trade operatives
Ambulance Drivers	men and women over 45
Messengers	motorcyclists and cyclists
Clerks and Storekeepers	men over 45 and women
Telephonists	men and women with switchboard training

In fact, at this point volunteers were coming forward quite readily for all of the various sections. Cole announced that he had a further 400 wardens in training and a similar number had joined the Auxiliary Fire Service. Within the senior

In the first months of the war the government concentrated on equipping the Auxiliary Fire Service with various types of trailer pumps that could be towed behind lightweight vehicles such as delivery vans and private cars. At the end of the first week of November 1939, eighty-seven light and sixteen medium, together with one heavy and two self-propelled pumps had been delivered to Fire Brigade Headquarters at Lancaster Place. Seen here in the cattle market car park in April 1941, the number soon rose to 139 trailers, 3 heavy pumps and an escape unit. *(Courtesy of* Leicester Mercury *and M. Tovey)*

As Auxiliary Fire Service units were recruited and attached to local fire brigades, the need for extra equipment became more pressing. Towed by small private and commercial vehicles, these small Beresford light trailer pumps were mass-produced and delivered to the AFS after September 1939. *(Courtesy of* Leicester Mercury*)*

management of the ARP there was a definite division of responsibility, in that the Chief Constable handled the recruitment and training of wardens, while the ARP Controller dealt with all other aspects of their work.

By the end of the first month of the war the City Council felt that satisfactory progress was being made with regards to the provision of air-raid shelters throughout the city. Plans were under way for a series of public shelters to be opened around the town which would be capable of accommodating over 4,000 people, while basement shelters in factories and other similar premises, that would hold a further 16,000, were being identified or built. The first of these public shelters to be opened, at the corner of George Street and Grosvenor Street, had mains electricity (which was transformed down to 12 volts) and was capable of sheltering fifty people.

During January 1940 work began on what was to be Leicester's largest shelter at the corner of Halford Street and Charles Street. Designed to hold 500 people it was to be followed by a second at the London Road end of Charles Street, capable of accommodating another 160.

Other shelters were built on the site of the old Burley's Lane omnibus station. In the latter months of the war, when it became apparent that the shelters were no longer required, the station reverted to its original use. A new set of platforms was built on the site which later became the city's central bus station (St Margaret's).

Things did not always go as smoothly as the engineers might have wished. In November 1940, at the height of the bombing and with the advent of winter, it was found that the newly dug underground shelters near the Lancaster Road fire station (in the grounds of the Wyggeston Girls School) were subject to flooding. Pumps and tubular heaters had to be installed to keep them in a habitable state. Electricity for lighting was supplied to these shelters by direct wiring from the Fire Brigade Headquarters.

Elsewhere in the city centre a basement shelter (equipped with bunks) was provided at the Leicester Guild for the Crippled in Colton Street. Shelters that had already been dug out in Town Hall Square were supplemented by surface shelters built on the car park in Wharf Street.

It was realised at an early stage that schools, by the very nature of their buildings, were eminently suitable for the reception and care of considerable numbers of people. Large-scale provisions were made around the outskirts of the city by the Education Committee for those who were caught away from home when an alert was sounded.

For home protection, 20,820 Anderson shelters were purchased by the ARP Committee and supplied to all householders in the city. Named after the then Home Secretary, Sir John Anderson, these sturdy shelters were to be a fixture in many back gardens for a number of years after the war had ended.

The problem of supplying a cheap and effective domestic shelter had been a matter of concern for the government for some time. In November 1938 Anderson commissioned engineer William Paterson to produce a suitable design. Within two weeks Paterson and his partner, Oscar Kerrison, had come up with the design that was to become familiar to millions of Britons.

Built in the grounds of the Wyggeston Girls School near to University Road, these shelters were unique in that after the war they were maintained by the Leicester City Fire Brigade as smoke chambers for training personnel in the use of breathing apparatus. *(Courtesy of* Leicester Mercury*)*

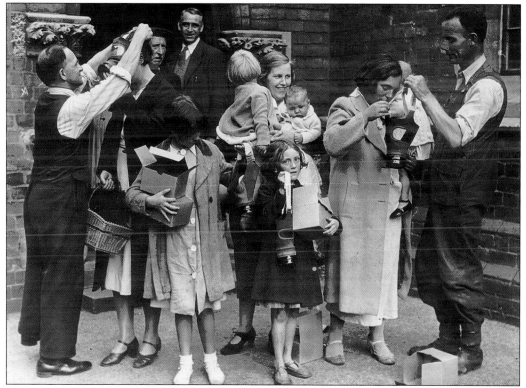

Children being issued with their respirators. The woman on the right of the picture has also been issued with one for the baby in her arms. *(Courtesy of Leicestershire Records Office)*

Buried in the ground to a depth of 3ft 4in, the basic standard shelter consisted of fourteen sheets of curved corrugated iron which formed a structure 3ft 6in high, 3ft 5in wide and 6ft 6in long, intended to house a family of four. Larger shelters, in varying sizes, were available to accommodate up to ten people. Once erected, the whole thing was covered over with 20in of garden soil to protect against blast damage. The allocation of these shelters was governed by a means test: to a family with an income of less than £250 a year, it was given free of charge; for those on higher incomes there was a cost, dependent on the size of shelter, of between £7 10s and £12 6s. In all, over 2¼ million Anderson shelters were erected across the country before the end of the war.

From an early stage Charles Keene came under considerable pressure from members of the City Council in respect of the costs of funding air-raid provisions for the city. There is no doubt that on the part of many of the older Council members this caution was attributable to them still being haunted by the spectre of the First World War, when expenditure was allowed to spiral out of control.

At the end of September 1939, three weeks into the war, Keene reported to the Council that spending on air-raid precautions during the previous five months amounted to £62,700, of which £45,000 would be defrayed by central government at Westminster.

During the previous week £4,600 had been paid out in wages to between 1,600 and 1,700 full-time ARP workers, which sum was well within the government recommendations. Of the 20,000 Anderson shelters delivered to the city, 18,000 had already been erected.

Sixteen First-Aid Posts were equipped and manned and the Traffic Commissioners had been asked to requisition 176 private cars for use as ambulances for these posts. (As time progressed G.F. Browne, the Commissioner of the Leicestershire and Rutland St John Ambulance, was appointed as First Aid Commandant for the Leicester ARP Services.)

Although the 'Committee of Three' was criticised by many – both inside and outside the Council Chamber – for the autocracy with which, on occasions, it acted, such criticism was for the most part unwarranted. Charles Keene and his two colleagues had been presented with a daunting task. Within a very short space of time they had to devise and control one of the most complex organisations that had ever been seen in the city. Working in unison with the Leicester

From the early months of the war various experiments were made in an effort to protect animals, particularly horses, from the effects of poisoned gas. In February 1941 the *Daily Telegraph* reported the proposal by the National ARP Animals Committee to trial a gasmask for horses. While the committee was aware of the difficulties involved, it advised that animals such as cats and dogs should be provided with specially constructed boxes, and caged birds covered down with a cloth soaked in either a weak solution of hypochlorite or permanganate. *(Courtesy of Leicester Mercury)*

For ARP purposes Leicester was divided into seven divisional areas. The city centre, because of the high density of property, was split into 'A', 'B' and 'C' Divisions, while the outer suburbs were: 'D', Beaumont Leys; 'E', Humberstone and Evington; 'F', Aylestone and Knighton; 'G', New Parks. *(Courtesy of Leicester Mercury)*

Emergency Committee they had to move swiftly and positively. There is no doubt that without their actions during the summer and autumn of 1939, adequate provisions for the safety of Leicester's citizens would never have been achieved so effectively.

Leicester was now divided into seven areas containing sixteen wards and under the direction of James Fyfe, the Housing Department Architect, ninety-six squads of men drawn from the building trade were allocated between them on a ratio of six teams to each ward. Every squad was comprised of two bricklayers, three carpenters, two joiners, one plumber and four labourers. Armed with specialist heavy equipment, it was to be their task to make safe properties which had been damaged in the immediate aftermath of an air attack. A pool of fifty men drawn from the Housing Department, together with almost a thousand volunteers, was put together as an additional source of labour.

Inevitably, in order to train and coordinate all of these groups, a complex series of exercises needed to be organised, mainly in the suburbs such as Humberstone and North Evington. Every weekend members of each of the voluntary organisations, ARP, St John Ambulance, Police, and the Auxiliary Fire Service turned out to deal with simulated gas attacks, air raids, and mock invasions. By the time bombs began to fall in reality on the city, the majority of the civilian population was adequately trained for most eventualities.

By the end of November 1939 8,000 men and women in Leicester had been enrolled into one branch or another of the Civil Defence organisation. Of these 8,000, just over 25 per cent – 2,159 – were employed full time and receiving payment for their services, the majority being first aid and medical workers along with newly enrolled volunteer firemen.

The Auxiliary Fire Service was one of the other most important organisations to be formed during the war along with the Women's Voluntary Service. Created under the Fire Brigade Act which was passed in 1937, the AFS was initially made up of volunteers over twenty-five years of age, who were attached on a regional basis to fire brigades throughout the country.

Three days after war was declared 400 men had joined the AFS in Leicester and within three months this number had increased to 1,859. This huge increase in manpower, which was reflected nationally, brought with it a logistical problem of equipping such an enlarged organisation. The problem was partially resolved by central government supplying each individual brigade with 'trailer pumps' that could be towed to the scenes of fires by private motor cars or tradesmen's delivery vans. Exactly 139 trailers, 3 heavy pumps and 1 escape unit were delivered to Leicester.

Winteringham decided that he would form a 'First Line' of full-time (paid) auxiliary firemen who would, supported by a nucleus of volunteers, be held in a state of permanent readiness. (At this stage the wage of a full-time AFS man was £3 per week.) A 'Second Line' would be made up of part-time volunteers, and have within its ranks a small percentage of full-time men.

The first turnout for the Auxiliaries in October 1939 was ironically not in the city, but to assist at a factory fire at Atkinson's dye works in Canal Street, South Wigston.

It is worth noting that under the Police and Firemen (War Service) Act 1939 the local authorities had the power to make up the wages of all police officers and firemen, who were away serving in HM Forces, to their full salary. Learning a lesson from the previous war, when this course of action had resulted in budgetary disaster, Leicester City Council decided that, in common with other employees of the Council, police and firemen would only receive a portion of their wages while away.

In October 1940, with the Battle of Britain won and Hitler in the process of launching his heavy bombers on England, the government took steps to ensure the safety of large factories and other premises which were considered to be targets.

The Fire Watchers Order 1940, made under the Defence Regulations 1939, directed that, during any period of attack:

1. all premises (except mines and quarries), in which more than 30 persons are employed
2. any building used wholly or in part as a warehouse of over 50,000 sq. ft
3. any saw-mill containing more than 50,000 cu. ft of timber, shall employ during any period of air attack, or when an air raid warning is in operation, a 'fire-watcher' to deal with any fires and summon such assistance as is necessary.

At the beginning of 1941 the ARP, on the instructions of the government, began to organise groups of householders in each street into 'fire parties'. During an air raid the fire parties, armed with the stirrup pumps being handed out here, were responsible for dealing with incendiaries dropped by enemy bombers. *(Courtesy of Leicestershire Records Office)*

This was followed up, at the beginning of January 1941 with a statement made to the nation by Herbert Morrison, to the effect that at the first sound of a siren it was no longer reasonable for householders and the owners of small business premises to abandon their property and expect that ARP Wardens would be responsible for its safety. A directive was circulated to ARP Controllers to put into place arrangements for 'fire watching parties' to be formed in every large urban area.

The wardens in Leicester (who now numbered 4,000) were instructed to organise householders in their area into groups of 7 (or fewer depending on the layout of the district). During any period of standby at least one of the houses was to be occupied by one or more persons who would have responsibility for the safety of the remainder of the group.

According to government advice every householder or business was to 'ensure that the trapdoor into the roof area was easily accessible, the roof space was to be cleared of any inflammable materials, and a half-filled bucket of sand or garden soil was placed in readiness on each floor of the premises'.

The advisory notices also carried the information that an enemy bomber was likely to drop over a target a 'Molotoff bread-basket', containing 100 incendiaries at a time, in order to saturate an area. If an incendiary fell through a roof into one

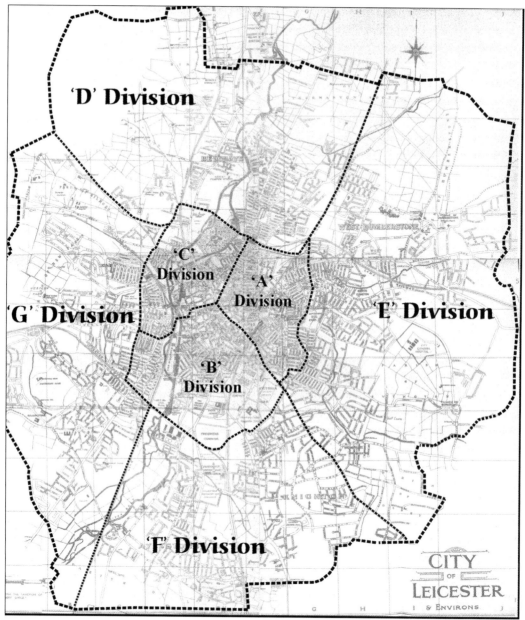

ARP divisions of Leicester city and the surrounding suburbs. The centre of the city comprised 'A', 'B' and 'C' Divisions, with dividing lines running along London Road, Belgrave Road, and High Street. On the outskirts 'D' Division encompassed the northern district from Beaumont Leys across to Belgrave; 'E' Division, Humberstone and Evington; 'F' Division, Knighton and Aylestone; 'G' Division, the west side of the city from Middleton Street to Gilroes Cemetery.

of the rooms, it was either to be smothered in sand, or covered with a wet blanket, then picked up on a shovel and thrown out into the street. Should the bomb have started a fire, or become lodged in the rafters of the house, it was to be extinguished with a stirrup pump. (As from January 1941 the use of rattles by wardens was discontinued and they were instructed to blow whistles as a signal that incendiaries were being dropped.)

The Warden Service immediately began to attempt to recruit 1,200 people within the city to form 'fire watching' and 'incendiary' squads. While the task was undertaken with a will, problems inevitably arose with regard to business premises – large and small. Almost every able-bodied man in the city was already recruited into one organisation or another, leaving very few to undertake fire-watching duties; also, the majority of shops in the town centre were staffed by young girls and women who were not suited for the task.

As Councillor Keene and Francis Winteringham addressed this latest problem, a temporary measure was set up during the first week of January whereby fifty police officers, assisted by Special Constables, patrolled the streets at night 'fire watching'.

The overall arrangements, put into place by the ARP Committee and managed by Francis Winteringham, stood the city in good stead during the intensive bombing attacks that the Midlands and Leicester were subjected to during the latter part of 1940.

In December of that year (after the major raids of November) Winteringham left Leicester to become Chief of the Birmingham Fire Brigade. He was replaced the following month by Errington McKinnell, a 36-year-old Northumbrian who had been in the Fire Service since 1923. Having served as the Head of Swansea Fire Brigade, McKinnell, prior to his appointment at Leicester, had been Home Office Fire Brigade Inspector for No. 1 (Northern) Region at Newcastle upon Tyne. Unfortunately in August 1941, after serving for only a very short time with the Leicester Brigade, McKinnell, much to the dismay of the City Council, was transferred by the government to take up the post of Fire Commander of No. 3 Force of the newly formed National Fire Service at Sheffield. The move as it transpired was relatively short term, and after the war McKinnell returned to resume his duties as Head of the re-formed Leicester City Brigade.

Francis Winteringham's departure from Leicester left the post of ARP Controller vacant. Because of his involvement in the recruiting and training of wardens, there was a presumption by many that the Chief Constable, Oswald Cole, would automatically replace him. Cole himself shared this supposition and in readiness began to divest himself of some of his other responsibilities. The elected members for Leicester, however, were apparently not so certain that Cole was the right man for the job. In a closed session of the Council, held just before Christmas 1940, a decision was taken to appoint Charles Keene, Chairman of the ARP Committee, to the post. The official reason given for this decision was that the Chief Constable had too many other responsibilities. During the first week of January 1941 a fifty-year-old retired naval officer, Maxwell Ritter, who had previously held a similar position at Willesdon in London, was appointed as Assistant ARP Controller at a salary of £750 a year.

CHAPTER THREE

The Phoney War: 1940

The military inactivity of the early months of 1940, before the German invasion of Norway and the subsequent dispatch of British and French Expeditionary Forces, led to the coining of the famous term the 'phoney war'. While it is true that prior to April and May there was little evidence of the events that were to come – Germany's invasion of Denmark and Norway followed by France and the Lowlands; the decisive 'Battle of Britain' and the subsequent bombing of British cities – the apparent lull did, however, give a much-needed breathing space for the organisation of an effective Home Front by the British government.

From an early stage it was decided that the 'volunteer spirit' of the previous war, when local authorities relied almost entirely on the public 'doing the right thing' by not emptying the shops of goods, and suppliers refraining from holding back stocks in order to keep prices up, was not going to suffice in the forthcoming conflict. Life had moved on over the last two decades in many ways. Technological advances alone – developments in the aircraft and armaments industries and improved communications systems – together with a public awareness that war was not the glorious business it had once been considered, meant that a different approach was going to be needed.

Conversely, certain other things had not changed. England was still not self-sufficient and continued in time of war to rely on the Atlantic supply lines bringing in materials from North America. Despite an unprecedented advance in transport systems, the armies on both sides were still to place enormous reliance on the horse for drawing guns and providing transport throughout the war. In January 1940, as in August 1914, the army began to requisition horses in the town and county for military purposes.

One of the earliest and, as far as the general public was concerned, most important developments during these early months was the phased introduction of rationing. It was realised by everyone, housewives and manufacturers alike, that supplies of food and raw materials were going to be restricted and that however unpopular, and often chaotic, the system was to become, rationing was inevitable. With petrol supplies already limited, on 11 March meat rationing was introduced.

The period immediately after Christmas 1939 was bitterly cold, seeing the lowest temperatures recorded in the county since 1895. At night the thermometer fell to between 12 and 18 degrees below freezing. While people skated on the ice at Groby Pool and Abbey Park, car cylinder heads cracked and Council plumbers dealt with an unprecedented number of burst pipes on the Saffron Lane estate. During the first week in February Leicester saw its heaviest fall of snow for a quarter of a century. (In the winter of 1916 soldiers were drafted in from the barracks to assist in clearing the streets.) Drifts 10ft deep closed most of the county roads and many outlying villages were completely cut off. With the points on the tram rails frozen solid, public transport in the city ground to a halt. A total of 800 men, including 400 'casuals', were brought into the city to clear the streets of an estimated 27in of snow.

In the depths of this biting weather the government announced that there was an acute shortage of coal, and cut back the supplies to merchants by 60 per cent.

Notwithstanding the problems caused by the weather, the City Council pressed on with its urgent programme of building public air-raid shelters in the town centre. During the last week of January work began on what was proposed to be – with a capacity to hold 500 people – Leicester's largest shelter, at the junction of Halford Street and Charles Street. Work continued digging out trench shelters in the Town Hall Square and fortifying basements identified in factory premises around the town.

In March came the first indications that the provisions being put in hand for the safety of the city were going to have to be paid for, in some measure, by the ratepayers. Timed to coincide with a statement in the Commons by the Chancellor, Sir John Simon, that air-raid precautions were costing the country £300,000 a day, Leicester Corporation announced that the rates were to go up by 6d to 14s 10d. ARP expenditure for the city, for the year 1939–40, was projected at £1.15 million. Even though central government would meet £905,000 of the costs, the ratepayers were going to have to look towards finding the remainder.

As time progressed and more pressures were exerted both nationally and locally on the population, the increases in the cost of living in most areas were absorbed philosophically by people and adjustments in lifestyles made accordingly.

Towards the end of March the question was again raised of how possible evacuees into the county were to be dealt with. In response to a Ministry of Health initiative, a questionnaire was circulated to all householders asking who among them would be prepared to voluntarily accept evacuated families into their homes.

The response, coming only a few months after the experiences of the previous year, when plans to relocate thousands of schoolchildren nationally had failed miserably, was not encouraging. In Leicester city less than 10 per cent of householders even bothered to answer the survey, and of those who did hardly any were prepared to volunteer. For the county, the return was even less promising. Of 4,200 forms sent out in Wigston, only 150 were returned. Similarly in Oadby, a mere 100 of the 3,000 circulated came back. In the outlying county areas it was worse; Melton Mowbray issued 17,000 and received back 120.

Once again the idea of securing accommodation voluntarily was, for the time being, set aside in favour of compulsory billeting should the necessity arise.

With the winter of 1939 passing into spring, the term 'phoney war' was for many becoming a reality. Although frantic provisions were being made by local authorities, and there was talk of further rationing, nothing tangible was happening.

March became April and people started to plan for Easter breaks; some even thought about summer holidays. Although petrol was now rationed, this did not make a vast difference to the majority of the inhabitants of Leicester, as relatively few possessed motor cars. The Chamber of Commerce declared that this year the Easter break would be extended from Good Friday to include the following Wednesday. Over the bank holiday period thirty-nine special and excursion trains (which was the equivalent to pre-war years), ran to various coastal resorts, and bus tours left the city for the vales of Derbyshire, Whipsnade Zoo, the Malverns, Cheddar Gorge and Skegness.

Not unexpectedly a result of the shortages being experienced was an increase in crime in the city. The Chief Constable reported as early as April that with food prices rising and under cover of the blackout shop breaking had increased dramatically since rationing was introduced. In one raid, on the warehouse of Vickers Mount and Co. in Bedford

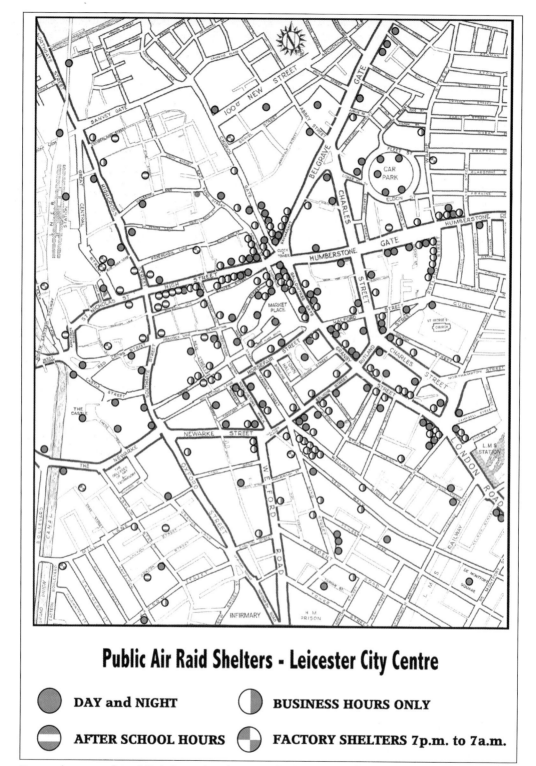

Public Air Raid Shelters - Leicester City Centre

⬤ **DAY and NIGHT**   ◑ **BUSINESS HOURS ONLY**

◒ **AFTER SCHOOL HOURS**   ✠ **FACTORY SHELTERS 7p.m. to 7a.m.**

Prepared as part of a public information document by ARP Controller, Francis Winteringham, during late 1940, this plan shows the extent of the arrangements for public air-raid shelters in the city centre. (*Author's Collection*)

Street, 1,344lb of sugar (the equivalent to 1,800 rations) together with a quantity of tinned salmon was stolen. Sold on the rapidly emerging black market the £50 value of this haul would have been trebled, and it is little surprise that the goods were never seen again. Later the same month a local motor dealer was convicted at Leicester Quarter Sessions of stealing 800 gallons of petrol worth £53 6s, from a warehouse in Syston and offering it for sale at 1s a gallon.

On a more sombre note, on Saturday 6 April all men of twenty-five years of age, not employed in reserved occupations, were required under the Training and National Service Acts to register for military service.

Errington McKinnell, Chief Officer, Leicester City Fire Brigade, January–August 1941. *(Courtesy of M. Tovey)*

Nationwide it was expected that around 300,000 men would now be required to register. In Leicester the figure was 2,300. Overall, this group would bring the number of men in the country currently registered for call-up to 1.85 million.

The following week saw Leicester's first casualties of the war. On 10 April a Hampden bomber crashed on to a house in St Denys Road at Evington, killing two of the crew and the occupant of the house.

If anyone was under any illusions as to the course the war was taking, these were dispelled on 9 April when German troops invaded Denmark and Norway, followed a month later by Holland, Belgium, and France.

The 1/5th Battalion of the Leicestershire Regiment, now under the command of Lt Col Guy German, together with the rest of the British Expeditionary Force were entrained as part of the 148th Infantry Brigade and set off for embarkation ports in Scotland. The first contingent under Lt Col German sailed from Rosyth on 16 April, followed two days later by a second unit under Maj A.H. Atkins from Aberdeen.

Norway was to be the first Allied setback of the war. Invaded by the Nazis primarily to ensure that the supplies of iron ore routed through Scandinavia continued to reach Germany, the administration of the country had been undermined by the leader of the Norwegian Fascist Party, Vikdun Quisling, who by delaying the mobilisation of the Norwegian Forces allowed the Germans to invade successfully. (Quisling, who was Minister of Defence between 1931 and 1933, was made Premier of Norway by Adolf Hitler in 1942. He was executed by the Norwegians as a collaborator in 1945.) The British and French troops hurriedly dispatched to Norway were not properly trained or equipped for warfare in Scandinavia, and after an abortive attempt to recapture the country a decision was taken on 27 April that the Allies should withdraw.

Several of the 'Leicester's' officers and men were killed during this short campaign, and on Monday 29 April the *Leicester Mercury* reported that their Commanding Officer, Guy German (later awarded the Distinguished Service Order), had been taken prisoner. He was to remain in a PoW camp for the next five years.

During the last week in October 1940, this French woman with her four children is pictured outside the DeMontfort Hall. Clasped in her left hand is a steel cash box containing what few valuables she has brought with her. *(Courtesy of* Leicester Mercury*)*

Men of the 1/5th Leicester's back from the snows of Norway. *(Courtesy of* Leicester Mercury*)*

After the Norwegian campaign the 1/5th Battalion was brought back to Scotland and re-formed at Hawick under the command of Lt Col C.B. Callander. In 1941 it moved to Ireland where command passed to Lt Col A.E. Wood. In 1942 the battalion was converted to a pre-Officer Candidate Training Unit and spent the remainder of the war at Wrotham in Kent.

On the evening of 10 May 1940, as German troops marched through Luxembourg into Holland and Belgium, Neville Chamberlain went to Buckingham Palace to resign his position as Prime Minister. In his place he recommended that Winston Churchill should be appointed as leader. Churchill also took over the role of Minister of Defence, thus ensuring that he maintained tight control of the three Armed Services. Chamberlain became Leader of the House of Commons, with a place in the War Cabinet.

In Leicester, with trains arriving at the railway stations loaded with men returning from Norway, the City Council redoubled its efforts to bring things to a state of preparedness for the air and gas attacks which were imminently expected.

Advice was circulated to all households as to the best way to erect and maintain the air-raid shelters that were appearing in everyone's back gardens. Residents were urged to make sure that the shelter door faced a brick wall or building in order to give protection against blast splinters; if this were not possible then some form of earthwork should be erected. The floor of the shelter needed to be between 2 and 4ft below ground level, while the roof and emergency exit at the back had to have a covering of at least 15 to 16in of earth or turf. Finally, a spanner was to be kept readily available at all times to unfasten the clip bolts on the emergency exit.

Surprise ARP exercises were laid on, with two 'Nazi parachutists' being dropped on Victoria Park, and the 'crew of a German bomber' arrested by police and ARP out in the county.

Sunday 5 May saw the largest coordinated Civil Defence exercise yet. Nationally, 70,000 volunteers were mobilised. In Leicester, where 1,200 wardens had now been recruited, a derelict house was set on fire in Grape Street for the AFS and Regular Fire Service to work on. Causeway Lane and Blue Boar Lane were closed off and a simulated air raid with civilian casualties was set up.

The drive to recruit more and more wardens continued with advertisements appearing in the newspapers, and for the first time declaring that 'responsible and active women, over twenty-five could be valuable in the service, not only as medical and nursing staff, but also as Wardens'. Meanwhile there was still a shortage of men in the 'Rescue, Shoring, and Demolition Section', and in the 'Roads and Sewers Repairs Parties'.

By now there were a total of fifty-five Wardens Depots and Reporting Centres, based in school halls and church rooms, in and around the city centre. The error of this was to become apparent, not only in Leicester but in other major cities around the country, when the heavy bombing raids that took place later in the year destroyed or damaged a huge number of them.

During May 1940 another organisation came into being which, in later years, was to be regarded for many reasons as something of an institution.

The fall of France early in the month resulted in what almost amounted to panic – at both government and public levels – that an invasion of Britain was just round

One of the first groups of Leicester men to volunteer for the Local Defence Volunteers, parading on the square at the Magazine Barracks in May 1940. (*Courtesy of* Leicester Mercury)

the corner. Rumours abounded that paratroopers, aided by Fifth Columnists, were about to take over the country; the Under Secretary for War, Lord Croft, sent Churchill a document estimating that an invasion force of some 100,000 airborne enemy troops should be anticipated. (In reality the Germans at this time had only 7,000 trained paratroopers.) During the second week of May plans were rushed through for a militia-style force to be created, and on 14 May the Minister for War, Anthony Eden, made a radio broadcast asking for men between the ages of sixteen and sixty-five to join the newly created Local Defence Volunteers.

At the end of the first day after Eden's broadcast thirty men had presented themselves at police stations in the city to register. While this was initially a very low figure (on the same day 200 men reported to county police houses and stations), the LDV, or Home Guard as it quickly became known, was always intended primarily to be a defence organisation for rural rather than urban areas. A notice was also issued by the Leicestershire War Emergency Committee to all ARP workers (of which at that point there were over 1,000 in the city), that they were already involved in essential war work and should not volunteer for the LDV.

However, during the next few days many more volunteers signed on for the Local Defence Volunteers, and by the end of the first week after its inception 1,300 men in the city and 3,000 in the county had come forward.

Initially the Leicester City Battalion of the LDV was formed, comprising four companies based at Aylestone Road power station, Western Park, Birstall Golf Club and Leicestershire Golf Club. Over a period of time other units were generated such as those belonging to the Leicester Tramways department and the LMS railway unit, made up of drivers, firemen, and guards employed at Beal Street motive power sheds.

Much to Eden's annoyance (over a million LDV armbands had been manufactured and were ready for distribution), a month after the formation of the Local Defence Volunteers Churchill insisted on the name being changed to 'Home

Home Guard soldiers, in an obviously posed picture, being instructed in the use of a Lewis gun, October 1940. In August 1940 the 1st City Battalion of the Home Guard received 950 denim suits, 490 rifles and 5 light machine-guns. The soldier at the back, whose denims are undone, is wearing a civilian shirt and tie: full uniform was still a thing of the future. (The side cap worn by the man next to him shows a very clear example of the Leicester Tigers 'Hindoostan' regimental badge.) *(Courtesy of* Leicester Mercury)

Guard'. One reason for the change was that the acronym 'LDV' was already being quoted as 'Look, Duck and Vanish!'

By December 1940 the battalion numbered 1,693 men which was to rise to 2,100 in 1943. Although the LDV began recruiting in May, the Leicester Battalion was not to receive any substantial supplies of stores or equipment until August, when an issue of denims, greatcoats, blankets and ground sheets, along with Home Guard armlets, arrived. The following month an issue of 156 battledress tunics

An LDV armband from May 1940. (*Author's Collection*)

supplemented the earlier denims. While uniform was distributed over a period of time, the rank structure in the early days remained rather loose. Commissions in the Home Guard were not authorised by the War Office until January 1941, and in fact it was April of that year before anyone in Leicester became commissioned. Prior to this, status was indicated by blue cloth bars worn on the tunic: a Battalion Commander wore three bars; a Company Commander two, with his second-in-command wearing one half bar less; and a Platoon Commander, one bar. It was not until February 1942 that 'Volunteers' became Privates. Although the Army's prime objective was to re-equip the regular soldiers returning first from Norway and Denmark, and then later from Dunkirk, arms were still issued to the Home Guard. The concept that the country was defended with broom handles is not completely accurate. In August 1940 the battalion was supplied with 490 rifles and 5 light machine-guns (which number, eight months later, had risen to 12). From photographs of the Home Guard training, these weapons would appear to have been Lewis guns and .303 calibre Brens.

The next blow to British prestige was the retreat of the British Expeditionary Force from France in late May and early June. The orderly groups of soldiers returning from Norway, many of whom still carried their kitbags and weapons, seen disembarking

Following the evacuation of 338,226 soldiers of the British Expeditionary Force from the French port of Dunkirk, men were sent to transit camps throughout Great Britain. The group seen here in summer 1940, probably at Glen Parva Barracks, is made up of men from many different units including the Leicestershire Regiment, and at least one Canadian (seated at table, centre). Many of these men would have been pre-war regular soldiers, as is evident by the Lance Corporal in the middle row who is wearing three medal ribbons, one of which carries a 'mentioned in dispatches' rosette. *(Courtesy of* Leicester Mercury*)*

from Leicester trains at the beginning of May, were replaced by the unfortunates who, among thousands of other troops, had escaped from the beaches of Dunkirk, forced to abandon their equipment and in many cases uniforms, in order to wade out to the boats waiting offshore to evacuate them. With a steady stream of troops making their way to the depot at Glen Parva barracks, the realisation came quickly to the people of Leicester that not only was the war now in full swing, it was not – for the time being at least – going well.

As a morale booster, hundreds of Leicester people were treated to a 'Back from Flanders' parade by men of the Leicestershire Regiment's Anti-Aircraft Battery.

Collar badge of the Leicestershire 'Tigers' Regiment. This shows a royal tiger surrounded by an unbroken laurel leaf. It varied from the cap badge in that the tiger's paw and tail were depicted differently, and the cap badge, which was open, was surmounted by a curved plaque and the word 'Hindoostan'. (*Author's Collection*)

In 1935 a decision had been taken that the Territorial Army would become responsible for anti-aircraft defences on the Home Front. At that time the number of men allocated by the TA to air defence formations was only 2,000; therefore, in order to achieve this new objective, a degree of reorganisation was necessary. In January 1936 selected battalions of the Territorial Army were converted, and three years later in April 1939 the establishment of anti-aircraft units was 96,000 men.

On 10 December 1936, as part of this restructuring, the 4th Battalion of the Leicester's, while retaining its cap badge and buttons, became part of the Corps of Royal Engineers, forming the 44th (Leicestershire Regiment), Anti Aircraft Battalion, Royal Engineers. It was incorporated as part of the 32 (Midland) Anti-Aircraft Brigade (TA) (2nd Division), together with other converted infantry battalions from Lincolnshire, Nottinghamshire and Staffordshire.

Having become an anti-aircraft battalion, very positive moves were made in the pre-war years to prepare the battery for operational duties. New drill halls dedicated to searchlight work were built: one as a battalion headquarters and two others, one for a company at Ulverscroft Road and a second for a company and a half at Brentwood Road in Clarendon Park; a fourth was built to accommodate half a company at Loughborough.

In the middle of June 1940 a government directive required local authorities throughout the country, as a precaution against invasion, to remove all place-names and signs that could be of use to the enemy. All over Britain the signposts were taken down or painted over. The Post-Master General gave instructions that the names on all post offices and telephone exchanges were to be painted out. The criterion was that 'a place-name must not be displayed where it can be seen from any vehicle slowly moving along a public highway'. As part of its endeavours to comply with this latest ordinance, the city's Transport Committee instructed that the name 'Leicester' should be painted out from all tramcars and buses.

Lord Mayor, Councillor Frank Acton, inspects a Guard of Honour of the 44th Anti-Aircraft Battalion of the Leicestershire Regiment in Victoria Park, July 1938. *(Courtesy of* Leicester Mercury*)*

Unlike the First World War, when almost every trade and industry in Leicester had flourished with wages taking an unprecedented upturn, business now became more unpredictable. Initially, in anticipation of a boom, industries such as the boot and shoe trade started Sunday working while hosiery and engineering companies implemented 24-hour shifts. A growing scarcity of materials within a very short space of time, however, brought a significant downturn to each of these industries bringing hardship for many workers. In July and August a decline in orders resulted in a slump in the boot and shoe trade. Unemployment rose and many men's wages fell to around 25s a week. The situation was exacerbated because, being in reserved occupations, their employers would not release employees to find work elsewhere in case an upturn in trade left the factories short of labour. Unemployment figures for August showed that 250 hosiery workers were currently idle.

Women operatives in the hosiery trade were particularly hard hit as they were among the first to be laid off. Even so, few of these women and young girls agreed to leave Leicester to work in other areas under the government redeployment scheme.

The City Council's Finance Committee now began to find itself under severe pressure with regard to the wartime allowances being paid to Council employees away in the Forces. Particular attention was drawn to the plight of teachers who were in the employ of the Council. A partial solution was arrived at when the Burnham Committee, sitting nationally to debate the question, decreed that teachers earning less than £5 a week were to receive a 6 per cent war bonus.

More urgently, the question of the employment of conscientious objectors in various trades and local government was becoming a moot point.

Members of the Leicester Hosiery Union and the boot and shoe employees, never sympathetic to the views of the conscientious objectors, were now refusing to work on the shop-floor with them. Consequently, many objectors were being dismissed from their employment in order to keep the main workforce in place. One of the largest groups of employees in the city were those working for the local authority, and it became apparent to the City Council that they were going to have to issue a clear policy regarding the matter. Initially, the Council declared that for the duration of the war conscientious objectors in their employment would receive no promotions or pay increases. This was extended during July 1940 to restricting the pay and allowances of conscientious objectors to those of a Private soldier, thus: an unmarried man 40s, and a married man 50s a week. The relevant child allowance would be: one child, 6s a week, two children 10s, three children 12s, and any additional children 3s a week.

Overall, considering how many men were being called up, the number of conscientious objectors in the city was relatively small. On 17 June when men of the 1911 Class (thirty-year-olds) were required to register for military service, of the 2,000 men who presented themselves on the Saturday morning, only thirty-five elected to go before the Tribunal to present their reasons for refusing. (After registering under the Military Service Act, men over thirty years of age were given the opportunity to elect to serve in the AFS or Police Reserve.)

During the summer months another group of newly formed volunteers was born which, as the war progressed, was to become increasingly important in establishing a further layer in the system by which the ever-present air-raid precautions could be enforced and refined.

'Neighbours Leagues' began to spring up all over the city. Their intentions were quite simply to go to the aid of vulnerable people, such as the elderly and infirm, in times of need. Two of the earliest to be established were in the Belgrave and Humberstone districts. It was not long before the potential of these groups was identified by the authorities, and they were being supplied with equipment such as stirrup pumps and other fire-fighting equipment.

One of the first tasks undertaken by the Neighbours Leagues was to organise the collection of materials in aid of the war effort. With a shortage of paper for the production of

START YOUR NEIGHBOURS LEAGUE

NOW !

A Neighbours League is a small group of neighbours, banded together for Mutual Help in times of Air Raids

For information write:-
THE CHIEF ORGANISER,
NEIGHBOURS LEAGUE,
CITY A.R.P DEPARTMENT,
24 HALFORD STREET.

At the height of the 'Battle of Britain', the Minister of Production, Lord Beaverbrook, launched his 'Saucepans into Spitfires' campaign. Together with the WVS the women of Leicester handed in their pots and pans for recycling. The slogan was 'bring out your aluminium!' *(Courtesy of* Leicester Mercury*)*

newsprint, now that supplies of Scandinavian wood pulp were no longer available, the *Leicester Mercury* was already offering a penny for every 3lb weight of old newspapers taken into their offices, and a penny for every 4lb of magazines. Through the Neighbours Leagues, Hugh Wilson, the Superintendent of the Corporation Cleansing and Waste Department, made an appeal for housewives to separate household rubbish and waste by putting paper and rags on one side for collection, and washing out tin cans which would be removed from the dustcarts by magnetic detectors for recycling. Additionally the WVS undertook to be responsible for the collection of aluminium throughout the city.

In July the Leicester Food Control Committee under Councillor Frank Acton set up a 'Fruit Disposal Committee', with a view to ensuring the distribution of surplus produce grown all around the city on ground that had been taken over for use as allotments. The scheme saw little success. Rationing was beginning to bite, butter was now only available on coupons, and supplies of sugar for bottling and preserving fruits were limited – few gardeners would consider that they had an excess of produce.

Not everything, however, was restricted: Leicester people were advised by the Food Committee to drink coffee which was not on ration, as opposed to tea which was 'in short supply'.

Intent on pursuing the aims of the war effort wherever possible, the Watch Committee gave permission for cinemas to open on a Sunday, provided that a levy of a farthing on every seat under 6d, and ½d on all other seats, was paid into a war charity fund by the cinema management.

As the year progressed and the fear of invasion continued to grow, proposals were made to evacuate children from England to the Dominions. (Both Canada and Australia, along with New Zealand, were already actively participating in the war. In June the first contingent of the Australian Imperial Force and the New Zealand Expeditionary Force – the ANZACS – arrived in England and from 21 June conscription came into force in Canada.) Following recent advice from central government, a meeting was held at Wyggeston Girls School in early July, when over a thousand Leicester parents applied for their children to be evacuated. Forms were already being collated by the city's Education Department and a large number of children had been examined by the Schools Medical Service. Completed application forms, received by the Overseas Reception Board in London, were being held back at the present time owing to shipping problems.

The question of evacuation was to be a difficult one throughout the war. Parents were desperate to ensure the safety of their children, while at the same time loath to receive refugees from other areas of the country into their own homes.

Evacuees from the east coast, on their arrival at Great Northern railway station on Belgrave Road, in August 1940. *(Courtesy of Leicester Mercury)*

Fund-raising, a basic element in the war effort, continued wherever it was possible to obtain donations. The Leicester and Leicestershire Patriotic Fund, recently formed as a joint city and county venture, was launched to provide assistance for the wives and families of men away in the Services. Additionally its aims were to supplement the work being done on behalf of men who were prisoners of war, provide comforts to men in hospitals, and to ensure that troops arriving at the railway stations around the city were cared for.

On 29 August at the height of the 'Battle of Britain' (10 July–31 October) the Mayor, Alderman George Parbury, launched the 'Lord Mayor's Spitfire Fund' in Victoria Park.

In 1940 the cost of a Spitfire was £5,000 and Lord Beaverbrook, who was Minister of Aircraft Production, proposed a series of funds be set up across the country to enable towns and cities to provide their own 'named' aircraft. The centrepiece of the Leicester Appeal, proudly displayed in the park, was a Messerschmitt 109 fighter, a victim of the 'Battle of Britain', that had been brought down over the south coast. (Beaverbrook was also making strenuous efforts to improve the country's heavy bomber strength in order to allow the RAF to continue operations against targets in Germany. By late September approximately 500 Boeing B17 'Flying Fortresses' were being flown to Britain across the Atlantic each month from factories in America.)

Between 8 August 1940, when it was opened, and 6 November that year the fund collected a total of £35,343 – sufficient to put seven fighters – *City of Leicester, I, II* and *III*; *Crispin of Leicester*; *The George Parbury*; *The Harry Livingstone* and *Brenda* into the air. (Brenda was named after the wife of a major contributor, David Burrows.)

With the ever present fear of invasion and air attacks, every suitable weapon was adapted for Home Defence. The two soldiers seen here are manning a .303 Bren gun – one of the most effective light machine-guns used by the British Army during the war. Note the spare magazine held by the man on the right. *(Courtesy of J. Baldaro)*

Since the middle of June German bombers had been penetrating the RAF fighter screen as far inland as the Midlands and at 10.15 a.m., on the morning of 21 August 1940, a single German aircraft, flying low over the city, dropped a stick of bombs along the length of Cavendish Road, off Saffron Lane, destroying a large number of houses and shops, killing six people and injuring another twenty-four.

In the next few months all the preparations put into place by Charles Keene and his colleagues were to prove their worth – the blitz had come to Leicester.

CHAPTER FOUR

Bombing of Leicester

From the earliest days of the war, steps were being taken by the government to effectively protect the Home Front and the British public from aerial attack. There were essentially two areas of concern: first, the threat to property and life from high-explosive and incendiary bombs combined with the effects that these would have on civilian morale and Britain's manufacturing capability; second, the more nebulous risk of poison gas being spread across the nation's cities.

German air power, tried and tested during the First World War, resulted in a specific Air Clause being inserted in the Treaty of Versailles after the armistice of 1918, preventing Germany from rebuilding its air force. The clause, however, neglected to prohibit the production of civilian aircraft. Consequently, during the interwar years, under the guise of rebuilding the German economy, there was an upsurge of air transport in the form of small (government-subsidised) airlines such as Lufthansa.

Flying and gliding clubs abounded, providing an ideal testing ground for designs of smaller, light aircraft. Through the membership of First World War flyers, the clubs also provided a valuable resource for training potential new pilots. (In 1930 the German flying clubs boasted a 50,000-strong membership.) It is worth noting that from 1926 onwards German pilots and observers were also being trained openly at Russian flying schools near Moscow and in the Ukraine.

Undetected by the Allies, firms such as Junkers, Heinkel, Dornier and Messerschmitt, financed by the *Reichsverkehrsministerium* (Ministry of Transport), were able to design and test as 'civilian transport' and 'single seater sports', machines that were to be the nucleus of a challenging new air force. A prime example is one of the most formidable of the German bombers, the Heinkel III, which derived from a fast mail plane built for Lufthansa in the early 1930s.

The Luftwaffe was officially established – with former First World War ace Hermann Göring as Commander-in-Chief – in 1935. The immediate strength of Hitler's newly revealed air force was 1,888 planes, including a bomber wing capable of undertaking strategic missions, staffed by 20,000 officers and men, who had previously been cloaked in flying clubs and as commercial airline and transport pilots.

With the outbreak of the Spanish Civil War in July 1936, Hitler perceived a unique opportunity to battle train his air squadrons, and offered help to General Francisco Franco, leader of the Nationalist Party. Hitler's airmen first took a background role, transporting troops and equipment, only later becoming involved in actual combat. In November 1936 the Legion Kondor was formed with aircraft and anti-aircraft batteries taking an active part in the war; German pilots and ground crews received a period of training that was to stand them in good stead three years later. (During the Second World War German anti-aircraft batteries – *Fliegerabwehrkanonen* (Flak) – were part of the Luftwaffe, unlike their British counterparts who were military units. It was in the bombing of the Spanish town of Guernica that Göring (who was also German Minister of Aviation), realised at first hand the effectiveness of aerial bombardment on civilian morale.)

One of the first bombs dropped just inside Cavendish Road from Saffron Lane, near to New Parks Road, rupturing a gas main in the middle of the road. This is near to George Dickens' newsagents (off picture on the left), and where the first fatality occurred in the roadway. The majority of those in steel helmets in the centre of the picture, working the two light jets of water (probably stirrup pumps), are firemen. *(Courtesy of Leicestershire Records Office)*

It was through these successes and other experiences gained by the German Air Force in Spain, that Göring – and consequently Hitler – became convinced that the Luftwaffe would constitute a critical element in attacks against targets on the British mainland and would provide a crucial precursor to any proposed land invasion.

Throughout the summer months of 1940 the air-raid sirens in Leicester were sounded on several occasions. The first time, in the early hours of Tuesday 25 June, was a false alarm although people took to the air-raid shelters. After three hours the 'all-clear' was sounded and people returned to their beds. The following night a second warning came as enemy aircraft passed over the city en route to another target. Over the next few weeks there were several similar night-time alarms, but no attack. When the first raid hit the city it was during the daytime and completely unexpected.

Wednesday 21 August was, so far as the citizens of Leicester were concerned, just another summer's day. The dull sky, overcast with heavy cloud, gave a promise of rain later. During the previous week large numbers of evacuees – women, children, and old people – had been trickling into the city from along the east coast, which was becoming the subject of enemy attentions. There was also news that men of the Leicester Tigers Regiment, who had managed to escape capture after the Norwegian campaign in April, were now safe in Scotland after making the final leg of their passage through Sweden. Those in the town who owned motor cars and delivery vans were becoming accustomed whenever they parked, in compliance with the latest Regulations, to locking their vehicles and taking the keys with them.

In Aylestone and Clarendon Park, people were going about their business in the usual way. Factory hands in the Co-operative Society's 'Wheatsheaf' factory, in Knighton Fields Road East, were turning out shoes in the main building, while newly trained women engineers in another section machined breeches and barrels for Bren guns. (The armament department was part of the British Small Arms (BSA) company, and many of the engineers had come to work in Leicester from Redditch in the West Midlands. A second subsidiary was operated on the opposite side of the town at Abbey Meadow Mills.)

Falling in a straight line along the roadway, the bombs caused extensive damage to property. Centre of the group, with a white band around his steel helmet, is the Senior Fire Officer. Men of one of the ARP Rescue Squads are beginning to clear away debris. *(Courtesy of* Leicester Mercury)

Although the bomber failed to hit any strategic target (the pilot was probably aiming for the nearby gasworks or the power station), the raid resulted in six people being killed and twenty-four injured. The handcart in the foreground, loaded with tools, belongs to one of the Rescue Squads. *(Courtesy of Leicester Mercury)*

When the air-raid warning sounded at 10.15 a.m. (one of the sirens was mounted at the Wheatsheaf), its undulating wailing was followed almost immediately by the crump of high-explosive bombs being dropped. Although many of those in the factory lived nearby, no one was allowed to leave to find out where the bombs were being dropped. The street that was hit – Cavendish Road, off Saffron Lane – was less than a quarter of a mile from the factory.

With the 'Battle of Britain' at its height, and RAF squadrons stretched to the limit dealing with the Luftwaffe's Me 109 escort fighters, German bombers were making determined efforts to slip through the fighter screen and hit daylight targets in the Home Counties and the Midlands.

There is reason to believe, however, that the lone raider who suddenly appeared out of the overcast sky over Leicester was in fact testing a new guidance system, and was reconnoitring the Midlands – possibly Coventry. Whatever his intended target (it has been generally presumed that it was initially the nearby gasworks or possibly the power station), diving as low as possible along the line of the road and its adjacent buildings (his identification markings were clearly visible from the ground), when he dropped his bombs the pilot was well aware that he was attacking a side street in a residential area. Eight HE (high-explosive) bombs were dropped in an almost perfect 300-yard line along the length of Cavendish Road, between Saffron Lane and Aylestone Road.

Every bomb struck home, and the damage and injuries caused were severe, although the area hit was relatively small. Six people were killed, the first being a man who was leaving George Dickens' newsagent's shop at 184–6 Cavendish Road (near Saffron Lane), having just purchased a morning paper. A further twenty-four were injured either by bomb blasts or falling masonry and rubble.

Four of the bombs fell along the centre of the road, destroying houses and shops and rupturing a gas main which caught fire, opposite the junction of New Park Road, between the Cavendish Wine and Spirit store and Hardacre's drapery shop. Two more of the bombs fell behind some houses further along the road, demolishing three of them and severely damaging others. The remaining two bombs, dropped at the opposite end of the street near to where it met Richmond Road, caused some damage to the nearby Methodist church, and made a large crater in the yard next to the Sunday school.

Although not the heaviest raid on the city by any means, the Cavendish Road bombing – along with the night of the Highfields attack – is probably one of the most clearly recollected by the citizens of Leicester. The fact that it came without warning in broad daylight served for the first time to bring home their vulnerability.

Only three weeks elapsed before the second attack; this time the target was on the north side of the city in the Gipsy Lane area.

As dusk fell over the city on Saturday 14 September, with the promise of a misty, moonlit night, it was exactly 8.54 p.m. when the sirens sounded to announce approaching enemy aircraft.

Families everywhere hurried to the safety of their Anderson shelters, dug securely into shallow pits in back gardens and covered over with topsoil to protect them against the splinters and debris caused by bomb blasts. The recent experience of Cavendish Road, and the information put out by the government that across the country, in the first half of the month, 2,000 civilians had been killed and 8,000 wounded by German bombers, ensured that the sirens were not ignored.

Once again it was a single aircraft that caused the damage, and the intended target was probably either the London Midland and Scottish, or the London and North Eastern Railway's lines, which intersected close to where the bombs actually dropped. (The fact that a mixed load of medium 50kg HE and heavier 250–500kg HE bombs was used in the raid indicates that the intended objective was either an industrial site or railway yards.)

Dropping over three streets, eight bombs demolished seven houses and severely damaged many more. The most badly hit was Essex Road where four people in one house, which took a direct hit, were all killed outright. This was where Charles Pulford and his adopted son, Jack Ball, lived with their wives.

Although five people were injured in the raid (in addition to the fatalities), there were several lucky escapes. One of those first on the scene to help bring the dead and injured out of the rubble, J.W. Farmer, a First-Aid Officer who lived nearby, told a *Mercury* reporter:

> . . . I was sitting at home when there was a loud explosion which shook the house and broke a few windows, I ran out and saw that a fire was starting outside a house on the opposite side of the road. I tried to put the fire out

thinking it was an incendiary bomb. When we discovered it to be gas burning we kept a stirrup pump at work to stop the fire spreading. . . . It was difficult to see in the dark what had happened, the flare of the gas lighted up three houses, the fronts of which had been blown away . . . I thought the occupants must be dead, I was astonished that they were only injured – and some not seriously at that. I gave them first-aid treatment and sent them to another house to keep warm and generally cared for until the ambulances arrived. . . .

In one of the houses that was hit a baby, Peggy Armer, was asleep in her cot when the roof and ceilings of the first floor of the house collapsed. The bottom of the cot gave way, dropping the child underneath it and protecting her from the rubble.

Favouring night raids over the Midlands, there was now a respite of eight and a half weeks before Leicester was again subjected to the attentions of the Luftwaffe.

During November the raids over Britain reached a peak, with almost nightly attacks on London and the Midlands. One of the reasons that the Germans were able to navigate to their objectives with such accuracy in darkness, was that their aircraft were equipped with the latest advanced radio navigation equipment. German technicians had come up with what was known as *Knickebein* (crooked leg). Based on the Lorenz System, which had been in use since the mid-1930s, it was a homing beam transmitted from occupied territory near to the Channel coast, along which bombers flew to their targets. It made night flying a much simpler and more accurate affair than previously. (A later version known as *X-Gerät* was used during the London Blitz.) A further advantage the Germans had in November 1940 was that the use by the RAF of radar-equipped night fighters was still in its infancy. thus allowing the Luftwaffe squadrons to operate impeded only by ground fire from anti-aircraft batteries.

Thursday 14 November 1940 saw the London Blitz's sixty-seventh consecutive raid since the first week in September, during which time an average of two hundred bombers had flown over the capital every night.

This was also the night when 449 German bombers, guided by 13 Heinkel IIIs (as pathfinders), of Kampfgruppe 100, subjected nearby Coventry to its heaviest raid of the war, dropping 400 tons of high-explosive bombs on the city and causing 1,350 casualties.

It was also the night that Leicester received its third visitation.

Soon after midnight, while residents on the south side of the city watched the glow on the horizon that was Coventry burning 30 miles away, an attack began on the west side of Leicester.

As the raiders flew over, a stick of bombs was dropped in a line from Kirby Muxloe, across the West End up to the cattle market on Welford Road. In view of the fact that there were no marker flares dropped, the intended target is debatable. The line of flight took the bombers across the LNER lines, and less than a mile north of the power station and the gasworks. Alternatively, it is possible that one of the German aircraft (owing to engine trouble or damage by anti-aircraft fire) was carrying a full bomb load and, unable to drop them over the designated target, unloaded them on the nearest city to Coventry before making a run for home.

One of the Building and Shoring Squads working on the precarious remains of a house in Cavendish Road. Someone has hung a defiant Union Jack flag from a doorframe on the exposed upper floor. *(Courtesy of Leicestershire Records Office)*

The mid-morning raid on Cavendish Road in August 1940 caused considerable damage to shops and private houses. *(Courtesy of* Leicester Mercury)

Whatever the reason, several houses and premises on the Hinckley and King Richard's Road side were hit, with two killed and ten injured. Squires bakery in Briton Street together with several houses in Latimer Street were damaged, and a bomb dropping at the junction of Fosse and Hinckley Roads left a large crater. The junction of Western Road and Briton Street also took a direct hit, demolishing the house that stood on the corner.

One bomb fell on the main stand of Leicester City Football Club in Filbert Street, which was severely damaged at the double-decker end, as were the roof, seating areas, kitchens, toilets, gymnasium and boardroom. Damage was estimated by the club at £15,000.

The night was not without some return, however. A Dornier bomber, which had taken part in the raid, was brought down at Burton-on-the-Wolds, near to Loughborough, killing the crew.

Without a doubt the single, most vividly recollected night of the war for those living in Leicester at the time was that of 19/20 November 1940, when the city was specifically targeted and subjected to a sustained blitz by the Luftwaffe.

Five nights after the raid on Coventry (and Leicester), Tuesday 19 November 1940 was selected by the Luftwaffe planning staff for another heavy bombing raid on the British mainland.

In the early evening 490 German bombers of Luftflotten 2 and 3 took off from bases in France and Belgium. While a limited number were given London as their target, the vast majority – 356 – were sent to Birmingham. A group of just over 50 were allocated secondary targets of which Leicester was one, and the indications are that between 25 and 30 bombers participated in the ensuing raid. Over the years there has been discussion as to whether or not Leicester was a specific target. It has been suggested that the bombers that hit Leicester could have been part of the main force attacking Birmingham. The later intelligence indicating that the German High Command was in possession of information concerning the city (and that Leicester was at the junction of a network of both rail and canal systems), as well as the sustained nature of the raid, makes this unlikely.

The weather conditions were ideal for the raiders. It was a dark night with very little cloud giving good visibility, and the weather for the time of the year was mild. Just after 7.30 p.m. enemy aircraft were reported approaching the city and ten minutes later at 7.40, when flares appeared in the sky, air-raid message 'Purple' was received.

Almost immediately incendiaries began to drop in a line from Aylestone gasworks, to a point east of the LNER station on Belgrave Road (still known locally by its old name of the Great Northern). The first buildings to fall victim to the incendiaries, at 7.46 p.m., were the churches of St John the Divine in South Albion Street, and Holy Cross in New Walk. (These marker fires were very close to Dover Street which was subjected to heavy bombing later in the night.)

At 7.49 p.m., with the air-raid message being upgraded to 'Red', the sirens were sounded, and a minute later the stand at the Tigers Rugby Football Ground on Aylestone Road was ablaze. This same burst of incendiaries also destroyed the nearby ARP mortuary; a makeshift one was later set up at the Aylestone Swimming Baths on Knighton Fields Road West.

The last of the markers dropped by the lead aircraft (timed at 7.56 p.m.) started fires in factories off Humberstone Road near to Wharf Street. One of the first to be hit was the premises of Hart & Levy in Wimbledon Street, where the flames were confined by the fire service to the first floor of the building.

Incendiaries falling at either end of Rutland Street next set fire to Freeman, Hardy & Willis' factory, and then to the nearby premises of Faire Brothers, which backed onto it in Wimbledon Street. (The top floors of Faire Brothers were set alight by the heat from the adjacent building.) These fires, which extended as far as South Albion Street, were controlled for about an hour and a half before an HE bomb, accompanied by further incendiaries, landed in the middle of the incident re-igniting everything again. At this point Faire Brothers was totally destroyed. The devastation here was such that the body of a fire-watcher, posted as missing during the night, was not found until final demolition and clearance work was carried out twelve months later.

The first high-explosive bombs (which continued to fall for the next five and a half hours until 1.35 a.m.) were recorded at 8.05 p.m., and ran directly across the city centre from west to east. Thereafter this area continued to be pounded by high-explosive and incendiary bombs throughout the remainder of the night.

Soon after 10 p.m. the area at the back of Granby Street was alight with the fires from Browett's Garage and Kemp's Ltd, in Dover Street. Here, a direct hit to the centre of the building caused a series of fires which, combined with the fire brigade's difficulty in delivering water into the fire, resulted in the collapse of the building. These were added to by Vice's printing works, in Calais Hill, and the factory of Moore Eady & Murcott Goode in Granby Street, which took direct hits, and where incendiary fires were held in check for some time by the fire brigade. Work here was impeded by the presence of an unexploded bomb, and the fact that high explosives were continuing to fall on the block while the emergency services were working.

One of the earliest fires of the evening was in the premises of James Lulham & Co., in Northampton Street. This incident was never officially reported to the fire control centre, which led to subsequent speculation that it could have been an accidental fire and might even have been responsible for guiding the German bombers to the city. From the outset, given the level of attention paid to such premises by the fire-guards, the possibility was remote and it was later decided that this was not the case. The premises were more likely hit very early on in the raid by incendiaries.

At midnight a direct hit on Grieves' machine-building factory in Queen Street, as well as the neighbouring Paragon works belonging to T. Venables Ltd, caused a fire which threatened the London Midland and Scottish Railway's grain warehouse in Samuel Street. The bombing of Grieves' premises was particularly unfortunate as the factory shelter took a direct hit, killing five of the workers taking refuge there and injuring fourteen more.

In Newarke Street the factory of James Hearth & Co. and the Providence Baptist chapel were completely gutted by fires and the flames were only just prevented from destroying the nearby electricity generating substation.

Several of the bombs that dropped failed to explode. One HE, early in the night, hit the town hall; it passed through the roof and came to rest in the basement, causing a small fire that was extinguished by a stirrup pump party. Great Central Street was also closed for several days after the raid while the area was cleared. Most problematic was the 'moving bomb' that fell into a bed of builders' sand in Queen Street – as the Bomb Disposal team removed the sand, so it buried itself deeper.

Away from the centre of the city, the suburbs did not escape the devastation. An early casualty came at 8.14 p.m., when a pair of semi-detached houses in Holmfield Avenue (off London Road) sustained hits. One bomb severely damaged two houses, while a second, exploding in the road, killed an ARP Warden who was hurrying to his post.

On the east side, the properties near Humberstone Road suffered badly. In a direct hit on Frank Street seven people were killed and eleven injured.

Another bomb hit Grove Road near to where it joined Vulcan Road and destroyed twelve houses. Ten people, including the local ARP Warden (whose body was not discovered under the wreckage for almost two weeks), were killed as well as fourteen casualties.

One person was killed by an explosion in Quenby Street, while nearby there was another fatality when houses in Bannerman Road were damaged.

'F' Division at Knighton was as badly hit as any other part of the outskirts. Ten incidents were reported, the most serious of which was a parachute mine dropping at the junction of Newstead and Knighton Roads. The resulting blast brought several fatalities and levelled two large houses in its path to the ground. Other houses in the surrounding area were badly damaged and a further eight dead and four injured were added to the night's total.

A short distance away two were killed and five injured in a direct hit on a house at the corner of Elms Road and Shirley Road, and two more died when another house sustained a direct hit in Knighton Road. The destruction of Hadfield's chemist shop on Allandale Road resulted in a further two deaths.

The devastation at the junction of Humberstone Gate and Rutland Street, where a sustained attack caused some of the heaviest damage in the city centre, 19/20 November 1940. The small cabin in the centre is the old 'City Coffee Stall', a well-known landmark of the time which miraculously escaped damage. *(Courtesy of* Leicester Mercury*)*

Southampton Street, looking towards Rutland Street, with the Odeon cinema on the left, 20 November 1940. Among the fire-fighters and ARP staff busy clearing up on the morning after the raid are a large number of onlookers. Those gathered on the right, at the corner of Wimbledon Street, are probably employees of Faire Brothers, whose factory was totally destroyed, and who have journeyed into town to find out the extent of the damage to their workplace. *(Courtesy of* Leicester Mercury*)*

Near to the LMS grain stores in Samuel Street, the area of East Short Street and Queen Street was heavily damaged. In the foreground is part of the rubble from Grieves' hosiery machine factory which sustained a direct hit at around midnight, killing five of those who were inside and injuring fourteen more. *(Courtesy of Leicestershire Records Office)*

A second parachute mine took out twelve houses, killing one person and injuring twenty-six others, when it landed at the junction of Tollemache Street and Sudely Avenue, off Abbey Lane. Had this particular mine (which in addition to demolishing the twelve houses damaged four hundred more) landed a short distance away it would have caused major disruption to the LNER railway system.

One of the less affected districts was Evington which reported twenty-six incidents of damage, but no casualties.

Irrespective of what took place elsewhere, it is fair to say that between 9.30 that night and 1.35 the following morning – when the last of the raiders left the skies over the city – it was in the Highfields district that the greatest carnage took place.

At 10 p.m., an hour and fifty-five minutes after the first high-explosive bombs hit the city, heavy-calibre HE bombs fell on the west side of Tichborne Street demolishing the boarding houses in Highfield Street, between Tichborne and Gotham Streets. Casualties in this densely populated area were heavy and this particular salvo alone claimed forty-one lives, including those of several members of the Royal Army Pays Corps who were billeted there.

Many people were trapped in this early blast, and from the outset the number of emergency teams sent by the ARP control centre was trebled. It was here that one of the lodging-house occupants – a man named Lasky – was buried for sixty-four hours before rescuers could dig him out. (The operation was effected under the most hazardous of conditions by tunnelling under a tottering 50ft-high wall and chimney stack.) Unfortunately, despite their efforts, he later died in hospital.

For the next three and a half hours this small area on the outskirts of the city centre was subjected to an incessant pounding.

Six people died and five were injured when a house at the junction of Highfield Street and Severn Street was destroyed. A few yards further along on Saxby Street a group of Czechoslovakian refugees was killed when the house in which they were billeted was hit. There were also remarkable escapes; one man, ignoring the sirens, went upstairs to take a bath and survived a blast in which five of his companions died. Rescue work here was further complicated by the presence of an unexploded bomb and ruptured gas piping that was on fire.

Almost simultaneously a salvo of high-explosive bombs dropping at the corner of Saxby Street and Sparkenhoe Street flattened all four corners of the junction. Several houses, the post office and the Wesleyan chapel – which was also the ARP depot – were destroyed. In this explosion a further thirteen people who were sheltering in the chapel died, and many others were injured and trapped. Although all the first-aid and rescue equipment was lost, the rescue squads who were out working among the wrecked houses escaped serious injury.

Personnel from Bond Street mobile First-Aid Post, who were sent to this incident, were in the process of taking over one of the houses that was still standing to use as an Emergency Dressing Station, when they too were hit, sustaining heavy casualties. Arriving on the scene shortly after midnight, a group of policemen (mainly

A parachute mine dropping at the junction of Tollemache Street and Sudely Avenue, off Abbey Lane, levelled twelve houses, killing one person and injuring another twenty-six. The mine narrowly missed the LNER railway tracks nearby. (*Courtesy of* Leicester Mercury)

When the first salvo of bombs dropped on the area of Highfields and Tichborne Street casualties were
high. Rescue crews here are digging a tunnel to release a man named Lasky, who was trapped for
sixty-four hours. Although eventually dug out of the rubble he later died in hospital. A Royal Army
Medical Corps Officer, holding wound dressings, and a Roman Catholic priest are among those
tending to the injured man. *(Courtesy of* Leicester Mercury)

detectives), who had been on fire-guard duty at Charles Street Police Station, began
helping with the rescue of those trapped. Half an hour later they were caught in the
blast at the Saxby and Sparkenhoe Street junction. Two of the party were killed
outright and a third, who was trapped in the fallen masonry, later died of his injuries.

The last of the bombers left the area at approximately 1.30 a.m. but the 'all-clear'
was not sounded until 4.04 a.m.

During this attack on Highfields there were many acts of extreme bravery by
members of the rescue teams and emergency services and some of these were
rewarded later.

ARP Warden John Higgott, an income tax inspector, went into one building
which had sustained a direct hit and was on the verge of collapsing, to rescue two
children whom he carried out, one under each arm, before returning to attempt to
extinguish a fire in the upper part of the premises. For this and other work during
the night, he was later awarded the George Medal.

St John Ambulance nurse, Ivy Marsh, who arrived with one of the mobile units,
was awarded a Certificate of Merit for the courage which she displayed in staying
with, and caring for, the injured policeman, Brian Hawkes, who later died in
hospital. In January the following year Nurse Marsh was also presented with a gold
watch by the City Police as a token of their esteem.

The official awards made in recognition of individual acts of bravery carried out
during what became known as the Highfields Blitz were the British Empire Medal

awarded to A.J. Harris, Civil (Defence Rescue Service) and Inspector J. Weston (Leicester City Police); and the St John Ambulance Service Certificate of Merit to Ambulance Officer L. Lee, Dr E.B. Garrett, Miss I. Marsh and Miss C. Wells.

When daylight broke the city was in a sorry state. A total of 550 houses were destroyed or seriously damaged while a further 4,200 had sustained varying levels of damage. Eleven industrial premises were demolished, and a further seventy-two unable to function. The total cost of the raid in monetary terms was estimated at £500,000. In terms of the cost in lives, 108 people had been killed – more than 60 of them in the Highfields Blitz – and 203 injured.

For the City Fire Brigade it had probably been the longest night in the history of the brigade. Fire Control recorded over fifty separate incidents which had been attended. Appliances with turntable ladders came into the city from Derby and Nottingham. Other assistance was drafted in from Loughborough, Hinckley, Melton Mowbray, Market Harborough, Oakham, Coalville, Wigston, Nottingham, Northampton and Peterborough.

ARP damage returns for the various divisions showed:

'A' Div.	Highfields	Very heavy damage
'B' Div.	Newarkes	Heavy damage
'C' Div.	Frog Island	Slight damage
'D' Div.	Belgrave	Slight damage
'E' Div.	Evington	Heavy damage
'F' Div.	Clarendon Park	Heavy damage
'G' Div.	West End	No damage

Adjacent to Highfield Street, Severn Street also sustained heavy damage. The wrecked vehicle is the remains of one of the Mobile First-Aid Team's ambulances, which was badly damaged during the rescue operations. *(Courtesy of Leicestershire Records Office)*

During the six hours that the raid lasted it was estimated that four parachute mines, approximately one hundred and fifty high explosive and several thousand incendiary bombs were dropped on the city.

Procedures were quickly under way to take care of the homeless. Gathered together by the Civil Defence at assembly points, they were taken by City Transport buses to the rest centres on the seven ARP divisions. These centres – established specifically for such a situation – had been activated at the first opportunity, and during the night and following day served in excess of 4,000 rations and refreshments. (They provided over a thousand breakfasts alone.) Depot canteens provided an additional 6,000 drinks and rations, and First-Aid Posts a further 5,500.

In order to begin clearing the debris and recover bodies the city Civil Defence Squads were supplemented during the day by parties arriving from Loughborough, Syston, Thurmaston, Wigston, Hinckley and Market Harborough. The organisation of these units was coordinated from Granby Halls.

By evening on Wednesday the 20th some semblance of order was restored. Primarily, all of the homeless had been found accommodation.

On the following night at about 8 p.m. an isolated, relatively low-key attack by a single aircraft was made. Two land mines were dropped, one of which reduced the engineering factory of Messrs Steels and Busks, in St Saviour's Road (along with much of the surrounding area) to rubble. (In the schedule of calls attended by the City Fire Brigade on the night of 19th/20th, a call-out to Steels and Busks, Temple Road, is shown. While it is possible that the factory received some damage that night and was hit a second time the following night, it is more likely that there is a date error in the schedule which was prepared later for the information of the Watch Committee.) The second mine, preceded by a flare, was dropped on Victoria Park, destroying the ornate pavilion situated near to London Road. The only casualties were five young women who were staying at the nearby YWCA on Granville Road.

While firemen were dealing with the resultant blaze, the sound of machine-gun fire was heard overhead as the raider was engaged by a fighter. It must be presumed that it was this that caused the bomber to break off its attack.

There was not another air raid on Leicester until, on the night of Wednesday 9 April 1941 at 9.20 p.m., the sirens announced the approach of enemy aircraft. In a swift hit-and-run attack, a stick of bombs was dropped over Ash Street near to Humberstone Road. This destroyed the Co-op grocery warehouse and the factory of George Green & Sons, injuring six people. As on the occasion before Christmas 1940, when the West End had been hit (on 14 November), it was again the night of a major raid on Coventry. It is very probable that the pilot for some reason could not make his drop over Coventry and decided to try for the main LMS railway tracks that ran parallel to Ash Street.

The great blitzes of the previous year were now a thing of the past and, for the Luftwaffe, raids over Britain were becoming more hazardous as time went by. On the day of this raid, in the early hours of the morning, a Heinkel III had been shot down in the county. In a dogfight with RAF fighters off the Welsh coast during the night six enemy bombers had been shot down; one of the squadron, damaged by the fighters and attempting to return to its base, came down near Peckleton. After two of the crew – the pilot and the navigator (who were later captured by a unit of the Home

Areas of the city and its environs that were subjected to the air raid on the night of 19–20 November 1940

On a plan of this scale it would not be practicable to show the fall of every individual bomb (even where they are known). For that reason the ☆ symbols are intended to show only the general location of where bombing took place. Similarly, no attempt has been made to show the estimated thirty H.E. bombs which failed to explode – such as the one that hit the Town Hall, and those that were cleared away during the days following the raid, from Great Central Street, Queen Street and East Park Road near to Fairfield Street.

Guard) – baled out, the plane crashed into the orchard of a farm near the village. The two remaining crew members, who were both injured, were also taken prisoner.

Before the end of the summer of 1941 there were to be two more raids on the city, one on the outskirts, and a second nearer to the town centre.

On the night of 17 May just after midnight, while a saturation raid was in progress over the neighbouring town of Nuneaton, bombs were dropped on the Braunstone estate. One fell in the gardens at the back of Cort Crescent, near the Anderson shelters, and severely damaged four houses, killing the female occupant of one and injuring six others. Premises in the surrounding streets sustained lesser damage.

While severe damage was caused to the houses in Cort Crescent, this picture illustrates the efficacy of the Anderson shelter. Very close to a direct hit, this shelter, buried in the ground and covered over with turf, has remained intact. The curved nature of its upper surface would tend to deflect a certain amount of blast. *(Courtesy of* Leicester Mercury*)*

Irreparably damaged by a land-mine about 8 p.m. on the night of 20 November, the Victoria Park pavilion was subsequently pulled down. The bomber that dropped the mine was driven off by an RAF fighter before it could inflict further damage. Five young women staying at the nearby YWCA hostel in Granville Road were the only casualties. De Montfort Hall in the background was unscathed. *(Courtesy of* Leicester Mercury*)*

Here again the choice of target is open to discussion. It is unlikely that in the circumstances Leicester was the bomber's designated target. If the pilot were returning with a part load of bombs, then it is highly likely that he would choose Leicester to jettison them. Whether German intelligence at this stage of the war was sufficiently well informed for them to be aware that the US 82nd Airborne Division had a camp on Braunstone Park within yards of Cort Crescent is debatable.

The final incident of the war, which sadly also resulted in a fatality, came two months later when, early on the morning of Monday 14 July in a short sharp raid aimed at the LMS railway station on London Road, a house in Conduit Street next to the sidings, a garage and some properties in Guthlaxton Street were damaged. While the disruption to the railway system was negligible, a lodging house on the corner of Conduit Street took a direct hit, killing the owner, Eliza Mott, and injuring seven others. A second bomb which dropped at the rear of the neighbouring properties caused some further damage.

The first air-raid warning for Leicester city was sounded on Tuesday 25 June 1940, and the last on Tuesday 20 March 1945; in between there had been in excess of 200 activations of the system. In the eight that signalled Leicester itself was about to be attacked, 255 houses were destroyed and 6,000 sustained some form of damage. A total of 122 people lost their lives and a further 280 were injured.

CHAPTER FIVE

Consolidation: 1941

In the aftermath of the previous year's air raids, the City Council and the people of Leicester took a deep breath and began to plan for the forthcoming year. Not unreasonably, attention focused on the probability of further enemy attacks and, with experience of what to expect, all of the available resources were directed towards the protection of life and property. While air raids on Great Britain were to continue for the rest of the war, for Leicester – although no one knew it – the danger was in fact virtually over. With the Luftwaffe's failure to win the 'Battle of Britain', Hitler's invasion plans had been abandoned by the German High Command – only one more air raid during the approaching summer was to be made on the city.

An early concern for the Council was how it was going to implement the Fire Prevention (Business Premises) Order which came into force on 29 January. The Order stated that 'it was the responsibility of all male persons to take turns of duty at the premises [where they were employed], and perform such fire prevention duties as may be allotted to them . . .'. (Duties performed outside normal working hours were not to exceed forty-eight hours in each month.)

With every available man and woman already involved in some form of Civil Defence work or other war-based activity, the requirement was an almost impossible one. The problem was not confined to businesses and industry. Schools with under three hundred pupils simply did not employ sufficient staff to comply with the Regulation. As an incentive to obtain extra volunteers, the Education Committee agreed to pay teachers on Fire Watch a subsistence allowance of between 1s 6d and 2s 6d, for each tour of duty. Already the costings which were being worked out to pay this allowance, on the basis of three people per building per night, amounted to an additional £19,485 a year.

In May the Regional Fire Prevention Officer, Lt Col S. Shephard, decided that a mandatory pool of Fire Watchers was to be formed and that the members, where necessary, would be sent to premises other than those in which they worked. The scheme was to be fully operational by the end of September. Every male between eighteen and sixty years of age and living within the city boundaries, unless specifically exempted, was required to register. (The main exemptions were members of the Observer Corps, merchant seamen, medical practitioners and certain disabled people.)

Somehow, as with most of the other wartime schemes, the Fire Watch Pool was made to work. By the beginning of August 57,000 men in the city had registered, and despite the fact that 90 per cent applied for an immediate exemption because they were already members of one or another of the Civil Defence organisations, sufficient manpower was eventually put together to provide cover for all the buildings and public places in the town. It was around this time that the official term of 'Fire Guards' came into usage.

Additionally the fire brigade placed throughout the city a series of 50-gallon water containers labelled 'Fire Services', for use in the event of water mains being put out of action during an air raid. Later, much larger 17,000-gallon static tanks were erected in

A party of evacuees arriving from the east coast. *(Courtesy of* Leicester Mercury*)*

Introduced into the British Army in 1937 to replace the older Lewis gun, the .303 calibre Bren light machine-gun became one of the main infantry weapons of the Second World War. An infantry section always carried a Bren as a support weapon; the Bren gun carrier was designed to ensure its mobility in the field and a mounting was produced in order that it could be used for aerial defence purposes. As the war progressed munitions workshops throughout the country produced the Bren under licence in order to keep pace with the army's ever increasing demand for the weapon. In Leicester a workshop was set up at the Co-operative shoe factory in Knighton Fields Road East. *(Courtesy of* Leicester Mercury*)*

the city streets, and pipes leading from the River Soar and the canal were laid along the gutters so that the brigade could pump water in the case of a mains failure. Neighbours Leagues in the suburbs took responsibility for the safety of dwelling houses. Working on the basis of one fire-watching party (made up of seven people) being responsible for 150yds of street or 30 houses, approximately 6,000 squads were formed.

The ARP Service was equally busy. Having learned – along with other cities – that it was a mistake to concentrate too many resources in the centre of what amounted to a possible target area, they looked to preparing public air-raid shelters on the outskirts of the town. Working in partnership with the Director of Education for Leicester city, Harold Magnay, a series of local schools became designated public shelters.

School	Facilities			
Melbourne Road School	Basement and brick shelters – accommodation for 200			
Hazel Street School	Infants' above-ground brick shelters –	"	"	250
Narborough Road School	Above-ground brick shelters –	"	"	380
Mantle Road School	Above-ground brick shelters –	"	"	200
Harrison Road School	Trenches in Little Rushey Fields –	"	"	600
Moat Road School	Outside underground shelters –	"	"	310
Green Lane School	Outside trenches –	"	"	270
Mundella School	One set of trenches –	"	"	400
Avenue Road School	Infants' shelters –	"	"	400
Caldecote Road School	Junior School shelters –	"	"	800

Similarly, the system whereby people who had been made homeless by bomb damage reported to sixteen 'Ward Welfare Centres' was discontinued. The problem produced by dealing with such people under a 'Ward Scheme' was that those taken in by householders from an adjacent ward slipped through the system and later missed out on many forms of aid.

Councillor Charles Worthington, the Chief Welfare Officer for the city, with Harold Magnay as his deputy, moved the staff out of these centres and relocated them in 'Divisional Air Raid Sectors'. Each sector was managed by a Welfare Officer whose responsibility it was to keep track of homeless families and ensure that they were given the correct levels of assistance. In the aftermath of a raid these centres would also be responsible for holding casualty lists.

The sectors and their associated welfare centres were:

'A' (Div.) Melbourne Hall   'B' (Div.) Narborough Road Public Library
'C' (Div.) Woodgate Library   'D' (Div.) Cossington Street Library
'E' (Div.) St Barnabas Road Library   'F' (Div.) Clarendon Park Library
'G' (Div.) 11 Glenfield Road

Before 1941 the ARP was based in twelve depots, all in adapted buildings and critically near to the city centre. In July 1941 a decision was taken to move the wardens to the outskirts of the town into four new purpose-built depots at an estimated cost of £8,000 each. Plans were submitted for the construction of the first two at Western Park and Rushey Fields, with provision for another two at Humberstone and Wigston Lane.

Not unnaturally the safety of those members of the public frequenting or working in the centres of all of Britain's main cities was a prime concern, not only for the Emergency Committee in Leicester but for the country as a whole. At the beginning of the year government officials conducted an inspection of the facilities in Leicester, visiting the shelters in Town Hall Square, Charles Street, the Leicester Guild for the Crippled in Colton Street and the surface shelters on the car park in Wharf Street (in future years this area of ground became Lee Circle). Later in the year the City Council sought advice from the RAF as to the best way in which it could minimise the aerial visibility of 'tram flashes', caused by the electric feed to tramcars working in the town centre and its suburbs.

During April the Home Secretary, Herbert Morrison, visited Leicester to conduct his own scrutiny of the city's Civil Defence and to inspect the facilities provided by the public air-raid shelters. (A Ministry of Food Order, issued in April 1941, permitted food to be served to members of the public taking refuge for long periods in public shelters. It is not clear how this was implemented, in other words where the food was brought in from – long-term storage of large amounts of supplies in the shelters would have been impracticable, and during a raid local authority canteens would be closed.)

At the end of March an amendment to the National Service Act 1939 permitted local authorities to put men who had been conscripted for the Armed Forces into either full-time ARP work or the Police Reserve, while still allowing them to qualify for the same war allowances as those who went into the Services. This gave the Council an

As each successive group of men received their call-up papers, large numbers presented themselves at the barracks to be registered. *(Courtesy of* Leicester Mercury*)*

Councillor Charles Worthington (1897–1970).
Born in Leicester and educated at Wyggeston Boys
School and Heidelberg University, he was
commissioned into the Royal Flying Corps in 1916.
Serving in Belgium and France as a fighter pilot,
Worthington was credited with several air victories.
In the years after the First World War he became a
successful businessman, among other interests being
a founding member of the Odeon group of cinemas
and the Managing Director of Worthington's Cash
Stores. Elected to the City Council in 1936, after
the outbreak of war he became City Welfare Officer
in 1940 with responsibility for the coordination of
post-raid aftercare, before taking over from Charles
Keene as ARP Controller in July 1941. *(Courtesy of
D. Seaton)*

opportunity to recruit badly needed manpower into the branches of the Civil Defence; it also had the added advantage that the provision included conscientious objectors who had previously been allowed to continue in their civilian jobs.

Once served with an enrolment notice, the person named was required to present himself to the relevant Civil Defence authority within three days. While most full-time Auxiliary Firemen over the age of twenty-five were 'reserved', after 30 June those who were only part time became liable for call-up.

Advertisements appeared for men to join the Civil Defence First-Aid Parties as drivers and stretcher-bearers at a weekly wage of £3 10s. With work in the building trade almost at a standstill (other than renovation and repair projects), tradesmen were offered full-time work in ARP Rescue Parties at between £3 10s and £4 5s a week. Working twelve-hour shifts, for those over thirty years of age, these were reserved occupations.

Lord Reith, the Minister of Works, lent an impetus to the campaign by offering to recruit a workforce of 100,000 men from the building trade, who would be exempt from call-up and would be required to go anywhere in the country on major building works (such as defence emplacements, airfields and army barracks) for the government.

On 8 July one of Leicester's most steadfast workers, Councillor Charles Keene, accepted the post of Deputy Regional ARP Commissioner and, resigning his position as ARP Controller for Leicester, started work in Nottingham. (Keene continued to live in Leicester and still maintained his position as a City Councillor.)

His place was taken, both as ARP Controller and Chairman of the Civil Defence and Emergency Committees by Councillor Charles Edward Worthington, who was head of one of Leicester's largest grocery chains, Worthington's Cash Stores Ltd.

In a year notable for the amount of legislation generated by Westminster, the Civil Defence Duties (Compulsory Enrolment) Order 1941 decreed in September that all males between eighteen and sixty (other than those already serving in the Forces or engaged in other specified organisations) would have to, before 6 September, enrol as members of the Civil Defence.

As in the previous war, a conflict was now arising between the needs of the army for men to feed the guns, and the needs of the munitions industry to supply those guns.

On 14 February 1941 Ernest Bevin announced that National Industrial Registration was to be brought in to enable the government to decide which factories were engaged in essential war work. The implications were obvious: those that were large enough to accommodate government contracts would continue to receive government support; those that were not would be absorbed.

In the meantime there was a concerted drive to bring female labour into industry. There is a popular misconception that the First World War brought about the industrial emancipation of women – this is not completely correct. Female labour was engaged during the First World War on the clear understanding (initiated and maintained by the Trade Unions) that after the war the status quo would be re-established – the men would be given back their jobs and the women would return to their place in society as home-makers and domestic staff. While this did not entirely happen, to a great extent women did return to their old pre-1914 situation. In 1941, however, both the manufacturing and service industries were far more amenable to the introduction of female labour than they had been a generation earlier.

Women working in the hosiery trade, which along with boot and shoe production was one of Leicester's main industries, were retrained as munitions and armament workers. (A prime example is the Leicester Co-operative Society, 'Wheatsheaf', boot and shoe factory in Knighton Fields Road East, where workshops were added on to the main buildings and local women were employed in the production of Bren guns.)

In early February women and girls, first from Corah's 'Wolsey Works' and Chilprufe, and later from Two Steeples in Wigston, were being retrained as engineers. By the end of the first week in March 120 were qualified to work the lathes and other machines of the engineering factories.

At the end of February the City Council, conscious that the standard of living of their staff, most of whom were on fixed wages, was slipping behind that of factory workers, initiated a cost of living bonus: 10 per cent for those on salaries of less than £300 per annum, 6 per cent on salaries of over £300 for the first £300, then 3 per cent thereafter, subject to the individual's salary and bonus not exceeding £500 a year. Overall the cost to the local authority was £15,000 a year which had to be set against a cost of living increase of 27 per cent since September 1939.

From the government's standpoint the situation was becoming more complicated by the day. In order to squeeze the last available manpower resources, reserved occupations were reassessed and new call-up dates announced for April, August and October. Leicester's two main industries, hosiery and shoe manufacture, found themselves under threat from both a shortage of materials and a potential loss of operatives.

In the hosiery trade the reserved age for knitters was raised from twenty-five years of age to thirty-five as from 1 April 1941. Foremen Charge Hands in shoe factories were told that they would no longer be considered to be in reserved occupations after October. The status of clerical staff would in future be discussed on an individual basis.

One of the considerations for Leicester's Chamber of Commerce was that, with the loss of so many shoe hands, smaller companies would inevitably be forced into bankruptcy. After some discussion the Leicester boot and shoe manufacturers, who were already suffering badly from a shortage of leather supplies, came up with a short-term plan to prevent manpower being drafted away from the shop-floor. Instead of laying off labour, which effectively meant 'giving away' men in reserved occupations, they would institute general short-term working. This meant that shoe hands would go into the factory every day for two or three hours, rather than working three full days a week, and signing on for the remainder at the Labour Exchange. It was, they knew, a very temporary solution to their dilemma; Ernest Bevin, the Minister of Labour, had already issued stern warnings that this practice would not be tolerated.

Those who were over the age for conscription did not escape the government's attention either; on Saturday 5 April an orderly queue of some 2,000 smartly dressed, middle-aged men formed up outside the Labour Exchange. On Bevin's instructions a comb-out was to be undertaken to find exactly who was doing what among the nation's white-collar workers.

Men aged between forty-one and forty-three, or more specifically those born after 31 December 1897 and before 6 April 1900, were required to register the precise nature of their current employment and whether they could be released from it. (Those in the boot and shoe industry were for the time being exempted from registration, as were members of the Home Guard.)

One week later, on 5 April, professional men such as bank managers, company directors and solicitors aged forty-one to forty-three were instructed to register at the Labour Exchange 'for consideration in respect of work of national importance'.

The attention of the government continued to focus upon the group in their early forties. In May it was decided that, under the National Service (Armed Forces) Act, men born in 1901 and 1902 must register for conscription. Once registered each individual's present occupation would be scrutinised and an assessment made as to which of them could be moved into other positions, thus releasing younger men for the forces. A rider was added that while being summoned for medical examination, those in this class, if required for the Armed Forces, would not be called up for some months.

Many men in this age group were already enlisted in one or another of the Home Guard companies in the city, and in an attempt to bring these units into line with the existing military organisation the War Office decided in April to grant the Home Guard the same rank structure as the British Army. On Wednesday 16 April an initial appointment of 301 commissions, including 247 Lieutenant-Colonels and Battalion Commanders, was announced.

At the beginning of December full conscription was extended to include those in the above age groups. With a view to providing a further 70,000 recruits during the following year, military call-up was further extended to include all males between eighteen and a half and fifty. Single women between the ages of twenty and fifty were also subject to call-up for the Auxiliary Territorial Service, Women's Auxiliary Air Force and the WRNS.

For the City Council 1941 was in some ways a watershed, in that for the first time they addressed the question of how, based on the presumption of an Allied victory, the problems of the postwar years were to be managed. It was already apparent that whether or not a victory was achieved in the next year, or in five

A newly formed ATS Company marching into Town Hall Square from Bishop Street, 10 September 1941. *(Courtesy of* Leicester Mercury*)*

years, a principal concern was going to be the rehousing of men returning from the war and their families. In the meantime they also had to address the immediate realities of what the war was doing to the local economy.

An increase in the cost of living and War Risks Insurance had already put up the cost of council house rents (many of which were being borne by women whose husbands were away fighting) by 1*s* 5*d* a week. War Risks Insurance was at this time costing the City Council £30,000 a year, of which £20,000 was attributable to the Housing and Education Departments. Additionally the Housing Authority was carrying a deficit of £16,000, of which £11,000 was down to the development plans for the New Parks housing estate, which was a major project to be built on the north-west side of the city. Reluctantly the Council agreed to a rate increase from 14*s* 10*d* to 16*s* for the forthcoming year, 1941–2.

In order to give both industry and the overall economy nationally a boost, double summertime was initiated on Sunday 4 May. It would, Herbert Morrison explained, 'enable factories to work double shifts in daylight, farmers to harvest for twice as long, and ships and railway yards to load and unload cargoes in daylight'.

Shortages of raw materials for the manufacturing industry in Leicester were becoming acute. In February the Ministry of Supply cut back supplies of leather by 25 per cent, causing serious disruption to local production. Despite their best efforts, employers began to lay off men, starting in the clicking rooms where the

HRH the Duke of Kent on the steps of the town hall during an official visit to Leicester in March 1941. The remainder of the group from left to right are: Lord Trent, Regional ARP Commissioner, William Cort, Lord Mayor of Leicester, and Charles Keene, ARP Controller. *(Courtesy of* Leicester Mercury*)*

shoe uppers were produced. In an effort to retrieve the situation it was agreed that Leicester manufacturers would produce 'National Branded Shoes' for men, women and children in medium-priced and cheap grades. The future supplies of other leather to a manufacturer would be dependent on how many of this type of shoe the factory produced. Problems in the hosiery trade were no less acute. In May 1942, under a new Essential Works Order, hosiery workers were given a guaranteed 48-hour week with an agreed national basic wage.

'Concentration of industry' in the hosiery trade was introduced in March 1941 in an effort to consolidate the large number of factories vying for government contracts. The basic plan was perfectly straightforward. Large manufacturers in the city who, in the view of the government, qualified as 'nucleus firms' simply absorbed their smaller rivals by a process of purchasing their government contracts from them.

A typical advertisement in the *Leicester Mercury* ran: 'Nottingham manufacturer of seamless half hose with basic production of 1,200 dozens per week would be pleased to collaborate with a manufacturer having a basic production of approximately 600 dozens per week. Advertiser has strong financial position.'

The scheme was a mixed blessing – many of those who were absorbed were quite happy to receive a cash handout and disappear into quiet obscurity. Others worried (with good reason) that an inevitable result would be the fixing of prices. It did, of course, release still more men for the ever-growing war machine. During March the Leicester boot and shoe manufacturers were asked to meet members of the Board of Trade to discuss how the system could be operated in their industry.

Shortages were not limited to these specific industries. Owing to a scarcity of paper the *Leicester Mercury* was reduced from sixteen pages to eight. A stockpile of coal was steadily being accumulated in the yards of local coal merchants in readiness for the next winter.

August 1941 saw a fundamental change to one of the organisations central to Leicester's war effort. There were, after the bombing attacks of 1940, in excess of one thousand fire authorities in England and Wales. Problems had arisen, when sending one brigade to the aid of another, over incompatibility of equipment, the use of different fire ground commands, rank structures and a host of other things. An obvious solution was that the service needed to be centralised, and a decision was taken to form a National Fire Service. (At the same time the responsibility for providing an ambulance service was removed from the fire brigade and transferred to the local authority, resulting in the subsequent creation of the Leicester City Ambulance Service.)

Leicester City Fire Brigade ceased to exist for the remainder of the war from 18 August 1941. All of the Regular and AFS personnel serving in the old brigade were amalgamated and became part of No. 9 Fire Area (Leicestershire and Northants). There were definite advantages in the change. As far as the organisation was concerned, standardisation of equipment, combined with a defined rank structure, made a postwar

Fire brigade crew on a 1930 model Merryweather pump escape, wearing anti-gas suits during a training exercise. *(Courtesy of Leicestershire Records Office)*

Operating fire escape at Lancaster Place fire station in a simulated gas attack. *(Courtesy of Leicestershire Records Office)*

reversion to borough and county brigades relatively easy. From the individuals' perspective, the former Auxiliary Fire Service men were brought into line with the old Regulars. Before the changeover an AFS man injured on duty through enemy action was dismissed after thirteen weeks and given the same disability allowance as a civilian. (Although the position in relation to firemen was addressed, throughout the war an ARP Warden was treated, for the purposes of compensation, as a civilian.)

To the complete amazement and frustration of the Leicester Watch Committee, in the middle of this restructuring they were told that Errington McKinnell was being arbitrarily removed from his post in Leicester to become Fire Force Officer of the Sheffield area. (The first intimation of the move came when the Chairman of the Watch Committee, Alderman Wilford, received a telephone call from the *Leicester*

Mercury.) While personal relations with McKinnell remained cordial (after the war he returned as Head of the re-formed Leicester City Brigade), a good deal of acrimonious correspondence took place between the Leicester Watch Committee and central government.

The newly appointed Fire Force Officer for Leicester was Arthur Netherwood who, though based at Leicester, did not personally take command of the Leicester section of the NFS; this role fell to the old Second Officer of the City Brigade, Arthur Cramp. Cramp, who had served in Leicester as a fireman since 1912, continued to command the brigade as Divisional Officer until his retirement at the end of the war in 1945.

While the authorities put into place all the provisions necessary for Leicester to survive any further incursions by the enemy, the average man and woman continued to play their own part in keeping the war effort going.

Senior schools in the city such as Wyggeston Boys, Alderman Newton's and Gateway supplied candidates to swell the ranks of the local Air Training Corps Squadrons, with a view to preparing them for the Air Force proper when they were old enough. At the end of January 1943 the Midland Command was the largest in the country with 30,000 cadets in 249 units.

As in the First World War, a Leicester and Leicestershire Prisoners of War Comforts Fund was established to liaise with the British Red Cross Society in monitoring the well-being of Leicester men held in enemy prisoner-of-war camps. (While a reasonable system was established for sending parcels and letters to men in German PoW camps, later, after the fall of Singapore in February 1942, it was not so easy with regard to those in Japanese hands.)

On Wednesday 16 April a huge crowd gathered in Town Hall Square to witness the presentation by the Lord Mayor, Councillor Cort, of a Regimental Colour to the Free French Forces' Chief of Staff, Gen Petit. Under a Guard of Honour provided by the Leicestershire Regiment, the crowd was treated to the sight of a full detachment of Free French troops being presented with the flag while their bugler sounded '*Au Drapeau*'.

Town Hall Square had for sixty-five years been the focal point for any civic or military events, and four months later crowds gathered again to watch as Air Vice Marshal Sir Oliver Swann took the salute for a march past of over five hundred uniformed women of the ATS, WAAFs and Land Army, as part of a major recruiting campaign to encourage women in the city to join the Women's Auxiliary Air Force.

From an early stage in the year restrictions on food supplies were becoming more noticeable. Meat was in short supply and the sales of bread and milk, while not yet rationed, were being strictly monitored. Spurred on by the Ministry of Food's 'Dig for Victory' campaign, golf clubs, in an effort to grow more home produce, gave over parts of their courses for planting up vegetables. Leicestershire Golf Club ploughed over 25½ acres (three holes), Birstall 23 acres. Rothley course, which had already turned parts over, now had sheep grazing on the uncultivated areas. Nationally the campaign was extremely successful and at the end of September 1941 Leicester had 4,500 wartime plots of land under cultivation as allotments. During the summer holidays students from Wyggeston Girls and Alderman Newton Schools organised 'farming camps' to supplement the efforts of the Women's Land Army and helped out on local farms around the district.

On 16 April 1941 the Lord Mayor presented a Regimental Colour to a unit of the Free French Forces in the Town Hall Square. The French officer on the saluting platform is the French Chief of Staff, Gen Petit. *(Courtesy of* Leicester Mercury)

Under another government initiative, the Council directed their attention in October to setting up a coordinated feeding scheme for schoolchildren. A central kitchen, allied to feeding facilities in ten schools, capable of serving 2,000 meals a day, was opened in Old Milton Street (near Bedford Street). This was an increase of 600 meals a day on the Education Committee's previous capability. Additionally, free milk was now provided in schools on a daily basis. In the case of a civil emergency, a further forty halls and other premises, each capable of producing 300 meals a day, were identified.

Shortages and the social upheaval caused by the war fuelled an increase in local crime. Unavoidably, supply and demand meant that the incidence of thefts and warehouse breakings soared. Tradesmen and shopkeepers were more than tempted to buy goods without questioning where they came from. In the late summer a driver was fined £5 (which in many cases amounted to the equivalent of a week's wages) for stealing four cartons of tomatoes, valued at £4, from the back of a LMS lorry and hiding them in an air-raid shelter. At the same time William White, a grocer in Lead Street was sentenced to three months in prison for receiving 57lb of margarine from a haul of 1,068lb that had been stolen from a depot in Henley Road.

Juvenile crime between April 1940 and April 1941 increased by 50 per cent. The frustrated Chief Constable, Oswald Cole – who attributed the increase to a combination of fathers being at war and mothers being at work – expressed the sentiment that 'adventurous trespass or the driving away of a car as an outlet of boyish energy might be overlooked, but in my opinion, children who despoil others' property should be whipped!'

In July, in a gesture of patriotic support, the hoardings around the Clock Tower were decorated with a huge 'V' sign; and on 2 July, at a cost of £52,000, Leicester's new bus station was opened at the back of Belgrave Gate, near Abbey Street.

The spectre of enemy attack was never far away and in August, with the summer drawing to an end, the first batch of the new 'Morrison table shelters' arrived in the city. Made of metal and intended for use inside a house, these shelters consisted of a steel cage with a mesh front and were just about large enough for two people to lie down in. (They were intended to fit beneath the stairs or under a large substantial dining table.) Costing £7 to buy, they were issued free of charge to householders earning less than £350 a year. The recommendation was to install them in a room facing a garden, as a bomb was likely to bury into soft ground before exploding, thus lessening the blast effect.

At the same time as the shelters were delivered, thousands of Leicester householders began queuing up outside the offices of the Inland Revenue in Albion Street to pay their first contributions under the newly introduced War Damage Insurance Act.

Surrounded by hoardings advertising National Service and ARP Services, the Clock Tower was from an early stage used to advertise promotions for the war effort. (*Courtesy of* Leicester Mercury)

On the evening of Wednesday 9 April 1941, an air raid on the east side of Leicester caused damage to Ash Street in the Humberstone Road area. Earlier that day, in the early hours of the morning, following a raid over the Welsh coast, a damaged Heinkel III bomber, attempting to return to its base, crashed at the rear of a farm at Peckleton near Desford. *(Courtesy of Leicester Mercury)*

The tail plane and part of the fuselage of the Heinkel III that crashed into the orchard of a farm at Peckleton in April 1941. Two of the crew, the pilot and navigator who baled out, were captured in the vicinity by members of the Home Guard. The two remaining crewmen who were injured when the aircraft came down were taken prisoner at the scene. *(Courtesy of Leicester Mercury)*

With winter approaching, the City Transport Department took a decision that as from Monday 1 September, because of a shortage of fuel, Corporation buses would stop running at 9.15 every evening. The department's fuel ration was 6,800 gallons per week, and it was currently using 7,700 gallons. During the previous winter curtailed services had allowed them to build up a supply of excess fuel, but this was now exhausted and a cutback in services became unavoidable.

The final initiative to be launched before the year's end was an appeal for people to chop down their iron railings and donate them as scrap for use in the building of tanks.

To promote the scheme, on Monday 8 September, following a Civic reception and a parade by the Home Guard, a Matilda tank, flanked by two Valentines and a scout car, appeared in Town Hall Square. The armoured vehicles spent the next two days touring the city and being displayed first on Spinney Hill and then Victoria Parks. Within a short time Corporation workers had collected 300 tons of iron railings from Latimer, Charnwood, Wycliffe and Spinney Hill Wards, while elsewhere a cull of 4,000 other properties, including churches, Corporation buildings, factories and such like, produced a further 16,000yds (just over 9 miles) of railings.

One of the most memorable events for the average person during this busy year was the murder by her husband of Nellie Thorpe, a 47-year-old factory hand, as she was walking home from work.

Nellie had married Thomas William Thorpe, a labourer employed by the Leicester Corporation Gas Department, in 1916. Thorpe, who was fourteen years older than his wife, was a heavy drinker with a violent disposition and the marriage, which was not a happy one, had ended several months before when his wife left him. After the separation Thorpe went to live with their married daughter at 3 Albany Cottages, off St Saviours Road.

On Monday 14 July Thorpe, who had been drinking, went to William Evans', factory in Lichfield Street where his wife worked as a shoe machinist. As Nellie Thorpe left the factory with another woman whom she was lodging with at 24 Brook Street, her husband followed them to the junction of Abbey Street and Belgrave Gate. He then jumped on her from behind, threw her to the ground and cut her throat with an open razor. In the crowded street several passers-by witnessed the attack, and a man riding past on his bicycle – Frederick Arthur Johnson, a clerk, of 11 Brentby Road – dropped his machine and grappled with Thorpe, disarming him as he attempted to cut his own throat. Nellie Thorpe died of her wounds in the ambulance on the way to Leicester Royal Infirmary.

At his trial Thomas Thorpe denied intending to murder his wife. He claimed that she had been having an affair for the last twelve months and that he had only intended to frighten her with the razor. Not unexpectedly, he was found guilty of murder and sentenced to death.

Thorpe was hanged at Leicester Prison three days before Christmas, on 22 December 1941. The last execution at the gaol had been that of Arnold Warren at the beginning of the previous war in 1914. Ironically, he also, following a failed marriage and a drinking session, had used an open razor, not to cut his wife's throat, but his two-year-old son's, on Western Park before failing in an attempt to kill himself.

CHAPTER SIX

The Middle Years: 1942–3

The weather at the beginning of 1942, accompanied by heavy falls of snow, was cold, dark and depressing. A flu epidemic, which held the city in its grip, almost brought the Transport Department to a standstill during the first week in January owing to the numbers of absent staff; at one point over eight hundred of the department's workers were ill. Late-night transport was cut back to a minimum, Sunday morning services were temporarily stopped, and in a further effort to cover the deficiencies those members of staff who were fit were asked, should the situation continue, to work an unbroken seven days once every three weeks. In spite of this, on one day alone 129 journeys were lost.

The war news meanwhile was improving. Having been shot down in action over France the preceding year, while serving with 92 Squadron, the pilot of one of the Leicester Spitfires, the *Harry Livingstone*, bought with money from the Lord Mayor's Fund, was now reported as being a prisoner of war instead of 'missing in action'.

Of the seven aircraft donated by the fund (there were others purchased with monies raised by private donations), two were shot down, three were lost in air accidents and two survived the war. The two that survived were *City of Leicester II*, which flew with 118 and 276 Squadrons before going to an Advanced Flying Unit, and *City of Leicester III*, which spent its time with a variety of Canadian, United States Army Air Force and Free French Squadrons, eventually being used for training purposes.

Together with the pilot of the *Harry Livingstone*, a further 350 servicemen from the city and 450 from the county were now in prisoner-of-war camps in Germany and Poland. The Leicester and Leicestershire Prisoners of War Relatives Association, along with the British Red Cross, worked tirelessly to maintain contact with them, sending letters and food parcels to supplement their meagre diet.

The lines of communication with the prisoners of war were kept open through the International Red Cross Committee. Parcels were first sent on board ship to a neutral country such as Portugal, then forwarded by rail to Geneva in Switzerland for onward transmission to the relevant PoW camps.

A typical Red Cross package would contain the following: a ¼lb packet of tea, bar of plain or milk chocolate, a tinned pudding, fifty cigarettes or tobacco, tin each of dried egg, margarine, vegetables, sardines or herrings, cocoa powder, processed cheese, condensed milk, preserve, sugar, biscuits, meat roll and a bar of soap.

By the end of the war in May 1945 over 20 million Red Cross packages had been sent to British and Dominion PoWs from twenty-five centres situated in England and Wales.

There were those in the city who tried to exploit the increasing shortages illegally. In February five local butchers, Albert Cant, Clifford Buxton, Frank Buxton, Roland Cleaver and George Daniell, were charged with 130 offences of slaughtering and selling sheep and cattle bought illegally from farmers in the district. The fraud enabled them to put the equivalent of 168,000 meat rations a

Throughout the war the collection of scrap metal for the production of aircraft and tanks was of major importance to the war effort. *(Courtesy of* Leicester Mercury*)*

week on to the black market. Each was given a sentence of one month in prison and fines ranging from £50 to £150.

Another Leicester man, Roland Wilkinson, a director of a company selling foodstuffs to a chain of NAAFIs (Navy, Army and Air Force Institutes) in the area, was sent to prison for twelve months for defrauding the Hawthorne Street depot in Derby of stock. The store manager also received a twelve months' prison sentence.

Hoarding of food was considered to be an equally serious matter, and was also dealt with severely. During the summer of 1942, in the middle of June, a raid on the sixteen-roomed home of Ernest Muddimer in De Montfort Street revealed a huge stockpile of foodstuffs concealed in his basement. This was to be the first case taken to court in the city under the Acquisition of Food (Excessive Quantities) Order 1939, and Muddimer was charged with hoarding a 4lb tin of brisket, two 6lb tins of ham, three picnic hams weighing 22½lb, 135 tins of fish, 95 tins of fruit, 117 tins of vegetables, 56 tins of meat, 50 tins of milk, 14lb of sugar, 46lb of tea, and 19lb of coffee. It was more than the majority of small shops could muster to put on their shelves for sale, and Muddimer was fined £128 with £30 costs.

On New Year's Day, following on the heels of the previous year's search for scrap metal, the Council stepped up the pressure on people to sort out for recycling those items that before the war constituted rubbish.

People were made more and more aware of what the shortages meant in terms of production. Fifteen tons of scrap metal would build a tank. Aluminium saucepans could be melted down for air frames. (Unfortunately, it was found that much of the aluminium kitchenware handed in was not in fact suitable for building aircraft.) The loss to the nation of rubber supplies, following Japan's entry into the war in December 1941, resulted in housewives being asked to hand in such things as rubber corsets, wellington boots, hot-water bottles and so on. Old clothes and rags, sorted to one side, went into the production of haversacks, field dressings, camouflage nets, and a host of other items. Women were even asked to separate out meat bones (Sunday joints were a thing of the past, but housewives could buy bones from the butcher to boil down and make soup or stock with), which could be used in the production of explosives.

Paper was another prime need. Leicester Corporation asked householders to hand in as much waste paper as they could lay their hands on. Paper was needed to make maps, vehicle logbooks, packing cases, gun fuses. A mortar shell carrier could be produced from half a dozen novels. At the beginning of the year the Cleansing Department was recovering about 80 tons a week. In May this had risen to 150 tons and in order to keep up the momentum a shop, run by the 'Waste Paper Recovery Association', was opened at 16 High Street as a receiving depot.

An advertisement appeared in the spring of 1943, produced on behalf of The Utilization Co. Ltd, Waste Paper Merchants, Western Boulevard, asking for donations as part of 'Leicester's Great Book Drive' to collect 600,000 books – all for recycling.

Cities and towns throughout the country were now being encouraged, in an attempt to defray the costs of the war, to 'adopt' various warships, aircraft and army units. Beginning on Friday 27 January, Leicester set about collecting £3 million to enable it to adopt the battle-cruiser HMS *Renown*. The sum – required to keep the ship at sea for the next twelve months – was an ambitious one. However, in a similar project, Nottingham had recently raised £2.5 million, so it was thought that the target was achievable.

HMS *Renown* was a 26,500-ton battle-cruiser, launched in 1916, which had served with the Grand Fleet in the North Sea during the First World War. In the months prior to September 1939, in readiness for action once more, she was fitted out with a modern anti-aircraft battery, enhanced aircraft handling facilities and up-to-date gunfire controls.

If the ship's record was anything to go by, it was worthy of the efforts being made by the citizens of Leicester to adopt it. In late 1939 *Renown* was part of the task force that hunted down the German pocket battleship *Admiral Graf Spee*. In April 1940 she was involved in the abortive Norwegian campaign, and also fought an engagement with the German battleships *Scharnhorst* and *Gneisenau*. At the time the appeal was launched the battle-cruiser was serving with Force 'H', based at Gibraltar in the Mediterranean. (After the war HMS *Renown* served in home waters for a further three years before being sold for scrap in March 1948.)

'Warship Week' was opened in Town Hall Square (which was decked out 'regatta style') on 28 February by Admiral of the Fleet Sir Reginald Tyrwhitt. Throughout the following week, in a series of fund-raising events, the people of Leicester collected nearly £4 million to maintain the vessel during the coming year.

During the summer of 1942, in a combined effort between the city and the county authorities, a two-day event was held in Bradgate Park. The display opened on Saturday 20 June with an impressive review of armoured vehicles and

For children, by now used to the exigencies of wartime, riding in a Bren gun carrier was the ultimate treat. *(Courtesy of* Leicester Mercury)

ambulances, led by the bands of the Lincolnshire and Buckinghamshire Regiments. Using the hilltop position of Old John as a grandstand for the loudspeaker commentaries, the two-day battle was opened by fusillades of Bren and rifle fire, accompanied by artillery shells (blanks) fired from guns on the opposite side of the river. In fine seasonal weather, the Home Guard and Civil Defence organisations staged a 'mock battle' in the park for the benefit of munitions workers in the Midlands – many of whom were part of the workforce that had built the Bren gun carriers that rolled up and down the hills behind Newtown Linford. Huge crowds of spectators, mainly arriving on bicycles and on foot, blocked the surrounding access roads as they gathered to watch the 'British and German Forces' battle it out across the park, with RAF planes flying over at tree-top level dropping dummy bombs on 'enemy' positions. Very soon the spectators were treated to the sight of the 'Germans' in full retreat, routed by enthusiastic Home Guard troops.

Inevitably, the British forces triumphed, and on Sunday, at the end of the exercise, many of those present were allowed to pile into the Bren gun carriers (and any other available vehicles) to be taken for rides across the open parkland. Much to the delight of the crowd, the only unscheduled diversion occurred when a stray mortar shell fell into some dry bracken, setting the hillside on fire.

Flushed with the success of this impressive exercise, a short while later, on 10 August, the Leicester and District Home Guard (which now numbered in its ranks some 540 City Council employees) proudly presented itself for inspection by the Lord Lieutenant of the County, Sir Arthur Hazelrigg. Under the command of Col H.W.H. Tyler, a total of 4,500 men marched from Lee Street to Victoria Park for the review.

In a similar manner to the ATC Squadrons that were training youngsters of school age in readiness for the Royal Air Force, four Army Cadet Companies in the

After completing their basic training, recruits were put into the General Service Corps while awaiting transfer to a regiment. This group is eating a meal during an exercise at Leicester Racecourse in October 1942. *(Courtesy of* Leicester Mercury*)*

city and county, affiliated to the Leicestershire Regiment, were looking to the needs of those intending to join the army.

Divided into companies one hundred strong, the objective of the Army Cadets was to train boys of between fourteen and seventeen in readiness to enter the army or the Home Guard. In the city, No. 1 Company was the Leicester Cadet Corps attached to Motor Reconnaissance, Home Guard Company. The county units were: No. 1 Company (Leicestershire), attached to Market Harborough Home Guard; No. 2 Company (Leicestershire), attached to Quorn Home Guard, while the Rawlins Grammar School Company was attached to Charnwood Home Guard.

As part of the Leicestershire Regiment there was also a Young Soldiers Battalion. In the early days of the war, battalions of the National Defence Corps (not to be confused with the Local Defence Volunteers), were formed from First World War veterans and youths of eighteen and nineteen. These were later converted into Young Soldiers Battalions.

Owing to manpower shortages as the war progressed, many of the original Warrant Officers and NCOs in these battalions were retained. Reg Sgt-Maj Goddard had, prior to September 1939, spent twelve years as Drum Major in the Tigers, while Cpl Neal had been with the regiment for twenty-eight years. Orderly Room Sgt James Lincoln served with the 5th Leicesters for three years during the First World War, rejoining the National Defence Corps in May 1939. Born in 1877, he was now sixty-five years of age.

Conscription, meanwhile, continued to absorb both men and women into the ranks of either the Armed Forces or one of the Civil Defence organisations at an alarming rate. Men who were drafted into the army received six weeks of basic training in the General Service Corps before being allocated to a regiment. With the constant depletion of available manpower, an estimated 45,000 women of all ages in the city were now required to register and be trained by the Fire Service as Fire Guards in factories and premises where more than thirty people were employed.

In June the Chancellor of the Exchequer, Sir Kingsley Wood, announced that the war was costing the taxpayer £84,240,000 a week (of this amount, expenditure on the fighting forces and supply services accounted for £68,750,000 a week or just over £9,750,000 a day – up to June 1942 the total cost of the war had reached £8.6 billion). Locally the City Council, worried about balancing budgets, gave out its own figures.

For the coming year the Leicester Civil Defence Committee estimated that it would need to spend £88,000, which was £12,000 more than in 1941.

There would be a saving in one respect now that the AFS had become part of the National Fire Service which, under the revised arrangements, was subject to central government funding. However, a trade off was that the Council was now responsible for maintaining the city's newly formed ambulance service.

It was hoped that an on-going Air Raid Shelter Programme, costing a further £120,000, would be in part subsidised by Westminster, while £22,000 was required for the building of the proposed ARP depots.

A new mobile canteen, purchased by the Ontario District of Canada, being handed over to the NFS by the Canadian Commissioner for Trade, James Cormack, on Friday 7 October 1942. *(Courtesy of Leicestershire Records Office)*

A group of young soldiers of the 7th Battalion, Leicestershire Regiment, watching the final of a six-a-side football match being played at Stamford in December 1943. The young man at the far right of the picture presents an excellent view of the Tigers badge on his side (field-service) cap. *(Courtesy of Leicester Mercury)*

Members of the Young Soldiers Battalion of the Tigers Regiment on Boxing Day 1942, after eating lunch which was prepared and served by their NCOs. *(Courtesy of Leicester Mercury)*

The NFS established a large number of small substations around the city and its environs, where they based a mobile trailer pump and personnel. This group of men and women, pictured in 1943, were stationed at some garages in Andover Street, which were used as a substation. The depot was closed in 1944. *(Courtesy of* Leicester Mercury *and M. Tovey)*

With compulsory legislation dictating that an ever increasing number of Fire Guards be enrolled, it had become necessary to make some of them full-time operatives, incurring a further cost of £17,200. (In September 1942 there were 75 'Head' and 250 'Senior' Fire Guards. The personnel in street parties – who were all volunteers – numbered 48,000.)

Ironically, despite the money and effort being put into the system, the Fire Guards were unable to prevent a major conflagration at the City Football Club in Filbert Street. At the end of June, with Divisional Officer Arthur Cramp in command, the NFS was called to a large fire in the club's grandstand. Although the blaze was prevented from spreading to the newly erected double-decker at the Aylestone Road end of the ground, the main stand, built after the First World War, and which had already sustained bomb damage in 1940, was destroyed. In total the damage, which included the players' dressing rooms, kit and equipment, came to an estimated £30,000.

It is probably fortunate that by now the likelihood of an enemy air attack was minimal. The obsession with fire watching and the consequent 'command structure' that evolved along with it was becoming absurd. A system was now devised whereby, in order to prevent several people reporting a fire simultaneously to the NFS, it became the sole responsibility of the Fire Guard to do so. (At this time there was no '999' system – all emergency calls to the police or fire services were made through the public telephone system.)

Fire Guards were now divided into sectors under a 'Sector Captain' and linked to an NFS station. Sectors were subdivided into smaller 'party areas', each with an

General Service Corps recruits undergoing bayonet training, September 1942. *(Courtesy of Leicester Mercury)*

assembly point. When a fire was discovered, a member of the Fire Guard team was sent at the run to report the occurrence to the party leader at the assembly point. Here another Fire Guard was dispatched with a written request from the party leader to the Sector Captain, for him to summon the fire brigade. Having scrutinised the written request, the Sector Captain then dispatched a third Fire Guard from his own team, this time on a bicycle for expediency, to the fire station . . . at which point an appliance was sent to the fire. It was a system that in later years was to provide the material from which situation comedies were created.

Adding to the pressure upon human resources, the Home Secretary, Herbert Morrison, appealed for a further 100,000 men and women to join the NFS in order to staff the 2,000 stations now operating throughout the country. A total of 50,000 men were required to man the fire pumps, and a further 50,000 women needed as telephone operators, dispatch riders, cooks and canteen assistants (women did not attend fires or operational incidents). While these continual demands for more and more part- and full-time workers took on a surreal aspect, in actual fact most of them were somehow met.

During the summer of 1942 the outcome of the war was still very much in the balance. Germany had invaded Yugoslavia and Greece, and British troops (including men of the Leicestershire Regiment) had been evicted from the Greek island of Crete. Following the fall of Singapore in February, among those passing into the hands of the Japanese, forty-one Leicester men were reported missing or prisoners. On the Eastern Front the German Army had begun its summer offensive launching attacks against the Russians at Sevastopol and in the Northern Caucasus.

In a concerted effort to boost morale, on Sunday 15 June, watched by an estimated crowd of 10,000 people, 5,000 Leicester men and women took part in a huge United Nations Day Parade in Victoria Park. Military detachments, Civil Defence, ATS, Special Constables, WVS, British Legion, St John Ambulance, Boy Scouts, and munitions workers (dressed in green overalls) marched behind the band of the 1st Leicester Home Guard. On a saluting base beneath the flags of twenty-eight nations, including those of America, Russia, China, France and the Dominions, the Lord Mayor, Councillor Elizabeth Fry, accompanied by the Bishop of Leicester, the Chief Constable, Capt Fouquies of the Free French Forces and other dignitaries, took the salute.

August bank holiday weekend saw Leicester's LMS station on London Road once more crowded with prospective holidaymakers waiting for the special excursion trains that had been laid on. The government, aware that 'travelling used fuel', had issued warnings for people to stay at home. To underline the stricture, police patrols were instructed to stop and check all vehicles on the roads leading into holiday resorts. More than one car load of would-be Leicester holidaymakers was stopped and reported by the police for the misuse of petrol on the roads into Blackpool and Skegness.

Meanwhile, for those who stayed at home various entertainments were laid on. A funfair was set up on the Lee Street car park and a circus appeared at the cattle market. An 'Olympia Horse Show' was held on the City Football Ground and the Leicestershire Cricket Team played a Services XI on the Oval at Abbey Park. Fitness and drill displays took place in Victoria Park and a fête was held in the De Montfort Hall.

United Nations Day Parade, June 1942. The Lord Mayor, Councillor Elizabeth Fry, and other dignitaries on the saluting base in Victoria Park. *(Courtesy of* Leicester Mercury*)*

Towards the end of the year an incident at the Leicester Dog Stadium on Parker Drive (off Blackbird Road), brought to the forefront a seedier side of life in the city. At a race meeting on Saturday 24 October, following what amounted to a gang dispute, Frank Sykes, a 44-year-old 'dealer', was shot and killed by George Edward Buxton.

Buxton – a 38-year-old hosiery hand living at 19 Saxby Street – and Sykes had been in dispute for some time. On Saturday 17 October, a week before the shooting, Buxton, while talking to a man outside the stadium, was set upon and beaten up by a group of men – including one 'Tacker' Smith and a butcher with the apt name of Cleaver – both of whom were associates of Frank Sykes. Fights of this nature were a common occurrence at the dog track and the incident seems to have attracted little attention. Buxton managed to escape from the gang and ran to a house in nearby Somerset Avenue, where he told the householder, Albert Johnson, that the beating was connected to his involvement with a woman.

On Thursday of the following week George Buxton was in the Admiral Nelson public house, in Humberstone Gate, with a woman named Doria Lilian Draycott whom he had known for some years, when a group of men including 'Tacker' Smith came in. Buxton made to leave but was stopped in the doorway by Smith who grabbed him and said, 'we've got you!'

Buxton replied, 'didn't you have enough last week?' whereupon one of the group (an airman) said to him, 'we're going to spoil this [your face] for you next time'.

On the day of the murder, at about 5 p.m., Buxton went into the 1s 6d enclosure at the stadium in a dishevelled state and told an acquaintance that he had been involved in a fight outside in the street with Cleaver. A few minutes later Cleaver, who was carrying either a bottle or an iron bar, came in with Frank Sykes and seeing Buxton over at the corner of the course near to the traps, approached him.

Sykes said to Buxton, 'now then you . . .', and both he and Cleaver began hitting him.

Breaking away, George Buxton pulled a .45 calibre Webley revolver from his pocket and told his attackers to 'stand back or you get this'.

Sykes burst out laughing and Buxton fired a shot at him. Despite the fact that he had been hit, Frank Sykes then said, 'if you can't shoot no better than that, throw it away', whereupon Buxton fired a second shot into him.

At this point Sgt James Auld of the City Police, who had positioned himself nearby no doubt anticipating trouble, came into the ring and, tackling Buxton, disarmed him.

Sykes and a woman named Eileen Jones, an innocent bystander who had been hit in the shoulder by one of the bullets (it having presumably passed through Sykes' body), were taken by ambulance to the Leicester Royal Infirmary. For reasons best known to himself Frank Sykes refused treatment at the hospital, and discharged himself – an action which was to cost him his life. Later that same night he was re-admitted; one of the bullets, which had passed through his intestines, had caused peritonitis from which he died at 4 a.m. the following morning.

The result of the murder trial three months later was to say the least unexpected. The trial judge held that George Buxton, a widower, who had been discharged from the army as medically unfit, had been the subject of a gang vendetta and had shot Frank Sykes under extreme provocation. Ignoring the fact that Buxton, taking a heavy calibre revolver with him, had gone to a place where he knew that Sykes and

This group, including Dr E.K. MacDonald, the Leicester Head of Civil Defence First Aid Services, are shown outside the town hall shortly after the separation of the Ambulance Service from the Fire Brigade, 27 March 1942. In the background the old building line of Horsefair Street is clearly visible. (*Courtesy of Leicestershire Records Office*)

his associates could be found, and having first threatened the deceased with the weapon, then fired two deliberate shots into him, the judge directed that he was guilty of manslaughter.

The penalty was even more bizarre. Sentenced to a mere three months' imprisonment, having already been on remand in custody for most of that time, Buxton served a further three days after his trial before being released. For the wounding of Eileen Jones, he was bound over to be of good behaviour for a year.

Further evidence of the situation at the dog stadium during this time can be seen in a civil case for wrongful dismissal brought against the stadium management by Gordon Arthur Newberry in December 1942, while Buxton was awaiting trial.

Newberry had been dismissed from his position as a kennel lad at the stadium in 1941 for allegedly doping a dog. In fact, Newberry asserted, he had been approached by another kennel lad on behalf of local gangsters to dope a dog, and had refused. Now that he knew what was going on, but refused to participate, he could no longer be allowed to remain. Therefore information was supplied to the track managers that he was involved in criminal activities, resulting in his dismissal.

The following year Alfred Clewlow, an engineering turner of Barclay Street, was sentenced to nine months' imprisonment for attempting to bribe another stadium employee to dope a dog.

Christmas 1942, as the vicissitudes of war bit ever deeper, proved to be a low key affair in the city. A party was held during Christmas week at the De Montfort Hall for 1,200 local children (many of whom were still recovering from a particularly nasty measles epidemic that had swept the town during the previous month), the majority of whose fathers were away in the army. Meanwhile, there was not a cycle lamp or battery to be had anywhere in the city to light people's way in the blacked-out streets. Dealers bemoaned the passing of the trusted old acetylene lamps for which the elusive batteries were not needed.

Presents, donated by various charitable groups, including some from the American Red Cross, were given out to deserving children in the community through the War Charities Office in the Municipal Buildings, and provision was made to ensure that the children of men who were prisoners of war each received a gift.

The New Year of 1943 showed little sign of being less austere. The Chancellor declared that the war was now costing £14 million a day, and the public should expect to have to tighten their belts even further during the forthcoming year. (Sir Kingsley Wood was to remain in the office of Chancellor of the Exchequer for only nine more months. In September 1943 he collapsed unexpectedly at his London flat and died of a heart attack.) In a spring budget on 12 April he announced that, among other things, from now on cigarettes, previously sold at 1s for ten, would cost 1s 2d, and the price of whisky would rise by 2s 4d to 25s 9d a bottle.

In September 1943, for the first time, the government introduced the PAYE (Pay As You Earn) method of collecting income tax. Initially applied only to those who were paid weekly (which constituted a huge percentage of the country's workforce), it was sold as a revolutionary leap forward in helping the working man and woman manage their finances more easily. The Chancellor hastened to point out that 'if a worker falls sick then their tax is paid up to date, also if he [or she] dies, there is no claim on their estate for the same reason'. To the more perceptive members of the electorate it was also apparent that, by the same reasoning, during a time of war anyone unfortunate enough to be killed in action, while serving in the Armed Forces, would also not owe the government any income tax.

Other costs were also steadily climbing, nowhere more so than in the clothing shops, where, with goods only available against coupons, prices had risen dramatically. A man's raincoat that in 1939 cost 21s was now priced at 38s 4d; a pair of men's shoes had risen from 12s 9d, to 16s 4d a pair. The price of a lady's swagger coat that in June 1939 sold for 21s had now quadrupled to £4. At a time when the minimum wage for a serviceman had just risen from 17s 6d a week to 21s, these were viewed as substantial increases.

The excessive calls on labour, both male and female, were now causing extensive problems both in the manufacturing and service industries. At the end of January 1943 the Isolation Hospital on Groby Road was unable to accept scarlet fever cases because of an acute shortage of both nursing and ancillary staff. Not only was the hospital thirty-nine nurses short, but when there should have been twenty-six ward maids there were seven. Of eleven kitchen staff the number was reduced to five, and only seven domestic house-maids were left to do the work of eighteen. On the other side of the city the General Hospital was in a similar parlous state instead of a staff of eight midwives, they had two.

Since the outbreak of war, picking up where the Voluntary Aid Detachments had left off in 1918, sleeping accommodation and refreshments for services personnel

Accompanied by Deputy Controller Ritter, HRH the Duchess of Gloucester inspects men of the ARP units. The 'CD' badge is clearly displayed on Ritter's battledress blouse. Each man is wearing a shoulder flash indicating which branch of the ARP he belongs to. The one nearest, wearing chevrons on his arm, displays a DEPOP flash, the next AMBULANCE, and the third RESCUE. Divisional letters are displayed on the front of the steel helmets. *(Courtesy of Leicestershire Records Office)*

Gas casualty demonstration by the ARP in Western Park. *(Courtesy of Leicestershire Records Office)*

were arranged in the rest rooms of the city's railway stations by members of the St John Ambulance and the Red Cross, who provided an invaluable resource for the servicemen and women passing through Leicester at all times of the day and night. However, for those permanently stationed in the district something more structured was needed.

During late 1942 and early 1943 a rash of 'Services Clubs' and 'Services Centres', funded by a variety of individual committees and organisations, sprang up in and around the city centre.

One such – the Leicester Services Information Centre, 'for the provision of a common meeting ground for American, Dominion, and British Forces in Leicester' – was opened by Brig Gen Claud Thiele of the United States Army.

On Christmas Eve 1942 it was announced that a Services Club was to be opened by the Civic Advisory Committee in conjunction with the YWCA, on the second and third floors of Montague Turner's (gents outfitters) at the Clock Tower. The Leicester Civic United Services Club, as it became known, was funded in part by the Finance Committee of the City Council who spent £2,250 on the kitchens and first-floor facilities, with a promise of a further £1,000 for improvements of the third floor. Some of the other costs (£1,000) were met by the Leicester and Leicestershire Patriotic Fund. Unfortunately, while the club had a number of attributes such as a dining room, small dance hall and theatre (it was envisaged that entertainment would be provided), the lease did not permit sleeping accommodation to be arranged.

In February a 'TOC H' Women's Services Club appeared in De Montfort Street, and on 8 March the 'Capital T' Club for members of the services started up at 22 High Street.

As the war progressed increasing numbers of American servicemen, from the military camps which were appearing on the outskirts of the town, were coming into the city centre and by January 1944 they had, through the offices of the American Red Cross, opened their own American Forces Club in Granby Street. The 'US Red Cross Club', which spread over four floors, had a lounge, snack bar, dining room and sleeping accommodation and was just one of 220 such establishments across the British Isles. (In December 1943 the first contingent of American nurses arrived in Britain.)

A sailor tying up a supplies barge before unloading at the Belgrave Ordnance depot. Above the boat's name – *Taurus* – can be seen the War Department's distinctive 'WD' marking. *(Courtesy of* Leicester Mercury)

Men from the Royal Army Ordnance Corps unloading a barge at Memory Lane Wharf in July 1943. The barges, which had a crew of four, had the capacity to carry a 35-ton load. This barge, which appears to be crewed by naval personnel, is flying a Red Ensign flag just in front of the cabin near to the sailor standing on the side of the wharf. (*Courtesy of* Leicester Mercury)

Efforts to find ways of conserving much needed fuel continued, and at the beginning of 1943 the managers of municipal transport departments across the country were instructed that within the next six months they would be required to convert all their buses from petrol and diesel engines to gas.

For the manager of Leicester City Transport Department this was not going to be an easy task. While it was entirely possible for him to comply with the new requirement, drivers would need to be retrained. Also, as a gas-powered engine would develop only 60 per cent of the efficiency of a petrol or diesel engine, buses in the city would no longer be able to carry a full complement of passengers. An added problem was the considerable time lost by vehicles being taken out of service for refuelling, as one tank of gas would only take a bus 60 miles around the city routes.

From 21 June 1943 it was agreed by the Leicester Bakers Association, in an endeavour to cut down on the amount of fuel used in delivering bread, that the city would be divided up by the trade into zones, and bakers would only deliver to certain streets in the immediate vicinity of their premises. One baker managed to reduce his delivery round from seventeen streets to one, yet still retained the same number of customers. The Leicester Co-operative Society declined to participate in this scheme, but did agree not to accept any new customers.

In an early anticipation of the terms of the newly published Beveridge Report, in May 1943 the City Council introduced for the first time provisions for certain of its members to receive sickness pay. Brought in under recommendations submitted to the National Joint Industrial Council, the scheme provided for Council manual workers to be allowed four weeks' paid sickness leave in any twelve months. The resolution was not allowed to pass through the Council Chamber without some searching discussion. Opposing the scheme, Councillor Percy Russell declared that 'if a man was going to get the same money when he was away sick as when he was well, there would be a great temptation to malinger'. (The measures recommended by the Beveridge Report, published in November 1942, were adopted and formed the basis of the British postwar Welfare State. Family allowances were introduced in 1945, and National Insurance and the National Health Service were established in 1946.

As wounded British and American soldiers began to filter back into the city from the fighting in North Africa in the early part of 1943, the *Leicester Mercury* reported the arrival of a minor celebrity. Flt Sgt John Hannah VC (who, while stationed in Lincolnshire had married a girl from Oakham) had come to live in the city after being discharged from the RAF as no longer medically fit for duty.

In May 1943 HRH the Duchess of Gloucester paid an official visit to Leicester to open the newly built ARP depot on Western Park. Pictured outside the Lord Mayor's Rooms, from left to right: Cllr Charles Worthington (ARP Controller for Leicester city), HRH the Duchess of Gloucester, O.J.B. Cole (Chief Constable), Lord Trent (Regional ARP Commissioner). *(Courtesy of Leicestershire Records Office)*

Born in Paisley in Scotland on 27 November 1921, John Hannah joined the Royal Air Force in the summer of 1939, and in 1940 became a wireless operator/air gunner in 83 Squadron, Bomber Command. On 15 September 1940, on returning from a bombing raid over Antwerp, his aircraft was hit by anti-aircraft bombardment and caught fire. The rear-gunner and navigator baled out, but Hannah remained on board with the pilot and fought the fire inside the bomber, first with two extinguishers and then with his bare hands, being terribly burned in the process. For his actions Flt Sgt Hannah was awarded the Victoria Cross.

After a long period spent in hospital, he was returned to his squadron on training duties, but his health broke down completely and he was discharged on 10 December 1942. Certified as 100 per cent disabled, John Hannah was awarded a pension of £3 7s 3d a week. This comprised £2 7s 6d for himself, 9s 2d allowance for his wife and 7s 1d for

Dated 1942, this *Leicester Mercury* picture does not give the location of this group of officers of the Leicestershire Regiment, although from the annotation, 'Officers of the Leicestershire Regiment photographed by a *Leicester Mercury* Cameraman at a recent inspection', it is probably somewhere local. Front row, left to right: Capt G.R. Lièbert; Capt L.M. Oram (adjutant); Maj L.H.S. Mowbray; Lt Gen J.S. Steele, DSO, MC; Lt Col P.A.B. Wrickson (CO); Gen Sir Clive G. Liddell, KCB, CMG, CBE, DSO; Maj Gen W.M. Ozanne, CBE, MC; Brig J.M. Rawcliffe, MC; Maj W.E.H. Garner; Maj J.R.A. Nicholson; Capt A. Edwards. Middle row: Lt/QMS R.R. Ralph; Capt V.W.J. Roussel; Capt R.H.B. Eades; Capt L.G. Ablitt; Capt R.S. Clark; Lt J.C. Stevenson; Lt J.A. Brand; Lt L.G. Mayhew; Capt J.R. Dain; Capt A. Davis. Back row: Capt J. Cross (RAMC); C/F E. Donaldson; 2/Lt I.E. Wallis; 2/Lt P.G. Bligh; 2/Lt C.M. Moncrieff; 2/Lt J.S. Richardson; Lt H.R. Davenport; 2/Lt E.C. Dunkley; 2/Lt K.J. Ashbrook. *(Courtesy of* Leicester Mercury*)*

their child. The remaining 3s 6d constituted his pension as the holder of the Victoria Cross. Hannah died at Birstall on 7 June 1947 and is buried in St James' churchyard at Birstall.

Although as the war progressed the danger of an invasion was becoming less and less imminent, the Home Guard continued to maintain a high level of vigilance in the city and county. From the time that Anthony Eden made his momentous speech in 1940, asking for recruits to join the Local Defence Volunteers, the organisation had flourished. Almost a million and a half men flocked to join the Home Guard's ranks.

The 'Dad's Army' image of the Home Guard is in some ways accurate, and in others flawed. Comprised almost entirely of men who were either in reserved occupations, too old, too young or medically unfit for military service, they were a mixed bag. However, the level of competence that they achieved has often been

Men of the General Service Corps being trained in the use of Bren guns on Leicester Racecourse.
(*Courtesy of* Leicester Mercury)

underestimated. The majority of units trained hard with the weapons at their disposal – American P.17 and Canadian .300 Ross rifles (such .303 Lee Enfield service rifles as they had were withdrawn for issuing to regular troops), old Lewis guns, Thompson sub-machine guns and a few Brens – and achieved a high level of proficiency.

Where the Home Guard differed from the other volunteer organisations was in the fact that it was the only one that carried arms and was affiliated to the army. Although in Leicester there does not seem to have been any great problem, in other parts of the country there was a certain amount of friction between the civil authorities and Home Guard commanders. Some Home Guard commanders saw their companies as observers reporting back to the nearest army unit, while others considered that they were a fighting force with an active responsibility for national security.

The latter were constantly coming into conflict with the police, owing to their practice of setting up road blocks and checking the papers and identity documents of motorists and members of the public. (On occasions some Home Guards even demanded identification papers from patrolling policemen.) Accidents (sometimes fatal) occurred when motorists failed to stop for these road blocks and the Home Guards manning them opened fire on the offending vehicle.

On Sunday 7 March 1943 an unfortunate accident occurred resulting in the death of one of the Leicester Home Guard officers. Lt Jack Moffatt, Headquarters Company, Leicester Home Guard, twenty-three years old and living on St Saviours Road, was a member of a platoon which had gone out from the city to participate in a river exercise at Wanlip. Live charges containing gelignite were laid across the river on the Syston side of the water and were detonated as soldiers in canoes made the river crossing. After the exercise had ended it was found that one of these mines had failed to explode. Moffatt, a Home Guard explosives specialist, was left in authority by the exercise commander pending the removal of the charge. While crossing from one side of the river to the other in a canoe, Lt Moffatt accidentally collided with the mine, causing it to explode and kill him.

As the end of summer 1943 approached it was becoming more apparent that the tide of war was turning in favour of an Allied victory. In the East an entire German army had surrendered to the Russians after failing to capture the beleaguered city of Stalingrad, while British and American Forces landed first in Sicily before going on to invade Italy.

The mood of the public improved dramatically, and with the promise of fine summer weather Leicester's railway stations were once again crowded with eager holidaymakers defying government advice to stay at home. For those who did remain in the city during the summer holiday period, the City Council's 'Holidays at Home' programme of events was another full one. Bands and military parades filled the parks with sporting events, displays and concerts. In Abbey Park a team of US servicemen played an exhibition game of baseball. One surprised housewife at Thurcaston received a parcel of lemons, sent by her husband, Sgm A.A. Moon, from Tunisia. When she undid it she discovered that the wrapping was in fact a bloodstained Italian battle flag. The accompanying letter from her husband explained that the flag, captured by him during the fighting at Enfidaville in Tunisia, had belonged to a section of the Italian 'Centaur' Division. He had taken it from the body of a dead Italian who was lying beside a crippled tank. Having first taken the flag to the offices of the *Leicester Mercury*, Mrs Moon eventually handed it to the Red Cross for safe keeping.

Many families in the city and county received the best present imaginable when, just before the fifth Christmas of the war, a small number of Leicester men were among a group of wounded PoWs who were exchanged for German prisoners held by the Allies. The return of 479 empire prisoners, mainly seriously wounded or sick men, in exchange for 1,061 Germans took place under the supervision of the British Ambassador Sir Samuel Hoare in Barcelona. (Hitler insisted on a ratio of two German soldiers for every British prisoner.) Fourteen Leicester men, including Major, Lord Cromwell, of Misterton Hall at Lutterworth, were among those who arrived back in the city from PoW camps, mainly in Poland.

Christmas 1943 was made a brighter affair than in recent years by the appearance in Leicester shops of a limited supply of fresh turkeys for the first time since 1939. A new innovation was specially designed 'Christmas Air-Grams', which troops in various locations were able to send home to their wives and families. In one case, a card designed by a Leicester man, Cpl H. Leslie Tams (an employee of the Leicester Corporation Electricity Department), was chosen out of 3,000 entries by the Royal Corps of Signals to be their official Christmas card from North Africa.

CHAPTER SEVEN

Rationing

The basis of an early rationing policy by the British government in respect of almost all consumable goods from food to motor fuel lay in the experiences gained during the previous war. In August 1914, despite appearances, Great Britain was no longer the economic power that it had once been. By the turn of the century countries such as America, Japan and Germany had all overtaken Britain. Crucially, the 'empire' of Victorian days was no longer supporting the country's needs and Britain was turning more and more to goods imported from Europe and America. By 1900 English farmers were producing only 50 per cent of the meat, 35 per cent of dairy products and 20 per cent of the wheat consumed by the nation. Once the constraints of war began to be felt the nation had to tighten its proverbial belt and deal with a whole series of shortages.

These deficiencies were approached during the first three years of the First World War – between 1914 and 1917 – very much on a voluntary basis. There were few motor vehicles on the roads (although fuel was restricted from a very early stage) and much more open space, even in towns and cities, for people to grow their own produce. Leicester was as badly hit by the shortages as the rest of the country. Food kitchens were opened in the borough (Leicester did not become a city until June 1919), and by 1917 queues formed on a daily basis outside food shops. In August 1917, far too late to be effective, a Food Control Committee was established to manage the meagre supplies available in the town.

Even the inmates at the workhouse on Sparkenhoe Street (Hillcrest) did not escape the enforced economies. In the words of Councillor Amos Sherriff, when tripe was substituted for meat one day a week as a main meal, 'the manner in which the inmates have previously been supplied with food, there might not have been a war on . . . if tripe suppers are so good, then a tripe dinner will be much appreciated by them . . .'.

It was not until December 1917 that items such as sugar were officially rationed. In April the following year, meat and bacon also went on to ration, followed a couple of months later by butter and margarine.

The lesson of the First World War was very clearly understood by the British government – insufficient regulation between 1914 and 1917 had almost brought the country to its knees. Abroad, the deterioration in social conditions resulted in the Russian Revolution, and the collapse of the German war effort was directly attributable to shortages on the Home Front. Matters were not helped during the interwar years. No sooner had progress towards rebuilding the economy begun, than the worldwide Depression of the 1930s brought unemployment and further shortages from which few nations were able to recover. In September 1939 Great Britain was importing around 55 million tons of goods a year.

The adult generation of 1939 remembered clearly the vicissitudes of the latter years of the First World War, and for this reason accepted philosophically from the outset the reasoning behind the government's stringent policies when war once more became inevitable. Strict measures were put in hand from a very early stage to ensure that such resources as were presently available would be carefully garnered. Well before September 1939 ration books had been printed and held in readiness for distribution.

The first commodity to be restricted was petrol. In the years since 1918 there had been a huge escalation in the number of motor vehicles on the roads; consequently a circle of supply and demand was created which persisted throughout the war. The private motorist and businessman were almost immediately taken off the road while the use of military vehicles increased disproportionately, creating a need for more fuel for official use.

It was announced by the government that petrol rationing would commence on Saturday 16 September 1939. There is, however, a small local anomaly here, as one week later, on Saturday 23 September, the *Leicester Mercury* announced that 'petrol rationing begins today'.

Motorists were directed to report to their local post office or the taxation department from which they usually purchased their Road Fund Licences (this term was replaced in later years by 'Vehicle Excise Licence'), in order to register. Ration books would be in two separate, one month, issues covering the period from the middle of September to the middle of November. The books contained ration 'units' each of which was equivalent to one gallon of petrol.

The initial allowance was: cars up to 7hp – 4 gallons per month; 8 to 9hp – 5 gallons; 10–12hp – 6 gallons; 13–15hp – 7 gallons; 16–19hp – 8 gallons; 20hp and over – 10 gallons. Motorcyclists received a flat rate of 2 gallons a month irrespective of the size of their machine. In real terms the fuel ration allowed motorists to travel between 150 and 200 miles a month. (The average cost of petrol at this time was approximately 1s 6d a gallon.) Leicester City Transport warned that with immediate effect the local bus services would be reduced where their routes were duplicated by the tramways.

As the war progressed, following a peak in U-boat activities, the petrol ration was halved during the summer (July) of 1941. Allowances in fuel rations, as with most other products, fluctuated from month to month. Even after the war ended, while the situation eased considerably, the restrictions still existed, as the figures for August 1945 show: cars, 10–18hp – 15–18 gallons a month; 14–19hp – 18–24 gallons; over 25hp – 20–25 gallons. Motorcycles over 250cc were allocated between 6 and 7½ gallons.

It was very obvious that the most important, controversial and complicated commodity that was going to come within the government's purview was food. Under the newly created Emergency Powers and Defence Regulations, brought into effect on 5 September 1939, local authorities were directed to set up Food Control Committees to oversee local distribution. A combination of Council members and business interests formed the committee for Leicester:

Food Exec. Officer:	Lucas McEvoy	(Town Clerk)
Assistant:	John Finlinson	(Asst Town Clerk)
Chairman:	Frank Acton	(Deputy Lord Mayor)
Secretary:	H.T. Sharman	(Leics & District Grocers Ass.)
	H.C. Olorenshaw	(President, Leics & District Butchers Ass.)
	T. Preston	(Manager, Leics Co-op, Grocery Dept)
	A. Hendry	(Leics Branch, National Dairymen's Ass.)
	John Greasley	(Leics & District Master Bakers & Confectioners Ass.)
	Miss A. Laffin	(Co-op Women's Guild)
	Miss M. Brown	(Women's Voluntary Service)
	S. Anstee	(Club & Institute Union Ltd)
	Cllr F.T. Jackson	(Leicester City Council)
	Cllr Mrs Swainson	(Leicester City Council)
	Ald. Geo. Parbury	(Leicester City Council)

At the inaugural meeting of the committee, John Finlinson was able to report that ration cards (required by the beginning of October) were in store for distribution in relation to: butcher's meat, butter and margarine, bacon, ham, cooking fats and sugar. (Standard ration books for adults were a buff colour, those for children green. Supplementary allowance books for pregnant and nursing mothers were green, and clothing books when later introduced were red. In November 1941 pink books were issued for special items such as tinned fruit.) With a staff of a hundred clerks working flat out to prepare over 250,000 ration books, by 1 November Finlinson had 2,600 ready for an initial distribution.

In his first budget speech of the war, presented to the Commons on Wednesday 27 September 1939, the Chancellor, Sir John Simon, announced the first price increases of the war. Income tax was raised by 2s to 7s 6d in the pound (a 36 per cent increase), 1d a pint was added on to the price of beer, and 3½d on an ounce of tobacco. The price of a bottle of whisky rose from 12s 6d to 13s 9d, and sugar went up by 1d a pound.

A year later, on 21 October 1940, Simon introduced purchase tax on a range of goods. This caused a degree of ill feeling, not to mention a short-term loss in profits for many of the smaller traders in Leicester. On the date when levying of the tax came into force – and many a shopkeeper was trying to work out exactly how much, at 33⅓ per cent needed to be added to an item selling at 6d – larger department stores, holding more extensive stocks, were in a position to continue selling at a cheaper rate. The Leicester Co-operative Society took out advertisements telling the public that goods such as drapery, footwear, furnishings, stationery, wirelesses, hardware, hairdressing and pharmacy items 'held in stock prior to 20th October would not be subjected to tax so long as stocks lasted'.

Throughout the war supplies of food and equipment for the army were moved about the country, through the inland waterways system, to Royal Army Ordnance Corps depots such as the one at Belgrave. *(Courtesy of* Leicester Mercury*)*

One of the first commodities to be controlled was meat, which officially became rationed during the first week of January 1940. (Again there is some area of grey in this; a Ministry of Food national advertisement, published in some newspapers on Friday 8 March, declared that meat rationing would commence the following Monday, which was the 11th.)

The Food Control Committee issued the following instructions to Leicester's householders with reference to the new ration books:

1. Put your name and address on the counterfoil at the bottom of the meat page in your ration book.
2. Write on the inside cover of the ration book, the name and address of your butcher.
3. Take the ration book to your butcher, who will write his name and address on the meat counterfoil and cut it out.
4. As items are purchased, your butcher will cut out the coupons.
5. If you move to another district, you must submit your ration book to the local Food Office of the new district.

These instructions were to become more and more familiar as time went by and other necessities were included in the list of restrictions. Later in the same month, butter (4oz a week), sugar (12oz a week) and bacon were added.

Control of the meat ration was probably one of the areas where the government experienced most difficulty. Throughout the war black market supplies were almost continuously available for those who could afford to pay the price, and despite a series of prosecutions resulting in gaol sentences, the rewards still outweighed the risks that unscrupulous traders were prepared to take.

The initial meat allowance for an adult was between 1s 5d and 2s a week. Bacon was restricted to between 4 and 8oz. The situation was, where possible, alleviated in some small way, as in April 1940 when pork was temporarily taken off ration and the existing meat allowance was raised to 1s 10d a head. In September of that year, as supplies eased for a while, the ration was again raised to 2s 2d a week. This profligacy was later regretted when the amount of meat coming into the city slumped by two-thirds just ten days before Christmas, and the allowance was immediately reduced to 1s 10d. The shortage continued into 1941 when in March the quota fell first to 1s 2d and then to 1s a head for adults and 6d for children.

In August 1943, in a move aimed at conserving fuel, it was announced that the meat industry was to be 'rationalised' (a poor choice of words in the circumstances). As from the end of the month no more deliveries of meat by motor vehicle or horse-drawn van would be allowed. Cycle deliveries, however, could continue uninterrupted. While a prohibition on the use of motor vehicles is not unreasonable (the bakery trade had already voluntarily reduced their delivery system), it is difficult to see the logic behind extending the ban to horse-drawn vehicles. Locally, in areas such as Braunstone where the number of shops was limited, butchers were permitted to go to designated pick-up points on the estate for customers to buy directly from their van.

As the war progressed and an Allied victory became more certain, together with a decline in enemy submarine activity that alleviated pressure on supplies from America to Britain, Christmas 1943 saw the first significant improvement in the situation.

'Christmas Turkeys from Eire' was the advertisement in local and national newspapers. For the first time in four years the spectre of a bleak Christmas in the city was to be avoided. The Ministry of Food had purchased from farmers in Ireland, 500,000 turkeys and a similar number of fowls. A further 275,000 turkeys and 150,000 fowls had been acquired from Northern Ireland. (The fowls were in fact mostly hens too old for laying eggs that had been put into the Christmas trade as boiling birds, but after the recent period of austerity even these were readily welcomed by housewives all over the country.)

Furthermore, the first cargo of Canadian apples for years arrived at the British dockside to provide the sauce for the festive birds. (The following summer a sufficient consignment of bacon crossed the Atlantic, again from Canada, to enable the ration between July and September to be increased from 4 to 6oz a week.)

As with many other items, the end of the war did not bring an end to meat rationing, and in fact from the middle of May 1945 the situation with regards to meat, bacon and cooking fats deteriorated. Soap supplies also became scarce. (A 12oz packet of soap represented half a month's allowance.) The meat ration was reduced from twenty-four to twenty points (1s 2d worth), part of which had to be taken in corned beef.

The other staple of the nation's diet was bread which, although subjected to many restrictions over the years, managed to escape actually being rationed throughout the war. (In the postwar years, however, despite its best efforts, the

Despite the restrictions imposed by rationing it was necessary to find extra food supplies for refugees coming into the city, both from the east coast and the London districts. The meal being served here in November 1940 at one of the school halls in Clarendon Park consists of soup (1*d*), Exeter stew and vegetables (6*d*), rice pudding and stewed apple (2*d*). *(Courtesy of* Leicester Mercury*)*

government was forced to impose bread rationing between 1946 and 1948.) An example of the constraints imposed on bakers is shown in an address by Lord Woolton, the Minister of Food, which was given to the Master Bakers, Confectioners and Caterers in Leicester on the afternoon of Wednesday 18 June. The minister told them that, with immediate effect, the slicing and wrapping of bread was prohibited and the number of different varieties that they could produce was to be restricted. In an attempt to produce a common loaf across the country, the ingredients were also to be standardised and vitamin B1 added. (Later on, in March 1944, the use of barley in loaves was discontinued.) In an attempt to boost morale, Lord Woolton pointed out that while bread in Germany was rationed, as yet that measure had been avoided in England.

The production of confectionery was, as in the previous war, legislated against from an early stage. In July 1940 a prohibition was placed on the production and sale of iced cakes, and in September the manufacture of candied peel and other cake additions was banned.

Other items to be subjected to restrictions from the outset were butter, margarine, cooking fats and sugar, all of which were on ration by the end of January 1940. By the middle of summer 1940 a combined ration of 6oz of butter and margarine per head was in force. Cooking fats (not including dripping and suet, which were not rationed) were restricted to 2oz of animal fat or lard a week. September 1940, one year into the war, saw the butter ration dramatically reduced owing to restrictions on imports from places such as New Zealand.

Eggs, which were one of the few things that could be produced domestically by those householders adhering to the old tradition of keeping a few hens in their back gardens, began to be in short supply after about eighteen months. Feed and upkeep for the birds (where supplies of corn could be purchased) cost money, and the price of fowls for the pot had risen from 2s 6d to 5s each in 1939, and to 7s 6d in 1941.

On 30 June 1941 the Ministry of Food directed that any producer of eggs who owned more than fifty hens, could now only sell their eggs through the government's newly established Central Packing Stations. Eleven months later a new staple was added to the nation's diet when dried egg was put on the government menu. In an attempt to supplement the nation's diet, 12 million tins of dried egg – the equivalent to 144 million fresh eggs – were sent out to distribution centres by the ministry. Available from the end of June 1942, a 5oz tin was the same price as a dozen fresh (or as they quickly became designated 'shell') eggs at 1s 9d. Lord Woolton himself went on record as declaring that 'when scrambled or in an omelette, they [dried eggs] cannot be distinguished from the real thing'.

Distribution of the tinned egg was left initially to the grocer with whom the householder was registered. He was directed to base the weekly quantity allowed on the usual amount of fresh eggs supplied to the customer.

As the shortages became more extreme, supplies of fresh eggs diminished alarmingly. On 18 October 1942 new and more Draconian restrictions were imposed on the sale and supply of both fresh and dried eggs. Children would no longer receive their priority ration of shell eggs, but would instead be given a double ration of dried egg. A 'priority ration' of three fresh eggs per week was given to pregnant women, nursing mothers and invalids. A proviso (seldom met) was made that 'where possible' all non-priority consumers would be allowed one shell egg a week. Tins of the dried product themselves were now strictly rationed to one packet or tin per week, and where there was a priority-rationed child in a household, two tins.

Once more, in an attempt to alleviate the situation, another substitute was introduced. A limited supply of 'cooking grade dried egg' came on to the market at 4s 9d per 1lb.

Starting in 1941, a severe shortage of fish hit Leicester's shops. With such things as poultry and rabbits already at a premium, the empty fish slabs brought severe financial hardship to many of the dealers. By the end of 1942 supplies from the docks at Bridlington and Grimsby were non-existent and the only fresh fish arriving in the city came from Fleetwood. There were several reasons for the problem. Fixing of prices by the government and the commandeering of fishing trawlers for naval purposes were crippling the industry. As a consequence fishing was now almost completely restricted to coastal trawling in small boats that could only work during the daylight hours. Additionally, the few deep-sea vessels that were still putting out into the North Sea were constantly in danger of submarine attacks.

Many other items, probably not so essential to the survival of the nation, but equally important in making life less arduous, also became restricted.

In 1941 it was announced that the extra ration of sugar that had previously been allowed for bottling fruit and preservatives would no longer be available. (There was good reason to suspect that much of this 'extra ration' was being diverted into general domestic use.)

February 1942 saw the family bar of soap available only on coupons. Four months later sweets and chocolate were put on ration, while two months after that cheese was apportioned at 3oz for each individual.

In July 1940, with supplies becoming shorter every month, a National Milk Scheme was introduced. This directed that nursing mothers plus children under five, who were not attending school, were entitled to one pint of milk a day at 2d a pint. People in this group could claim their milk free if they satisfied one of the following criteria:

Joint income of the parents was less than 40s a week.
Income of a sole parent or guardian was less than 27s a week.
Head of the household was in receipt of public assistance, unemployment benefit, or supplementary old age pension.

After the scheme was launched the take-up everywhere exceeded the government's expectations. By the end of the second week in July 4,000 applications had been made to the Leicester Milk Office for cheap milk, and 700 for the free allocation. One week later, on 23 July, the office's overworked staff announced that applications for free milk had now reached 6,000, resulting in 1,500 permits a day being issued. This was merely a reflection of the situation across the country. At the beginning of the second week in August 1940, five weeks after the scheme was launched, it was estimated that 1,787,849 claimants out of a

These young soldiers from the Tigers Regiment, on a camp out in the country, have found a way of circumventing the feeding problem by catching their own food. *(Courtesy of* Leicester Mercury*)*

possible 3,758,000 had already applied. Of these, 464,905 were receiving free milk and 1,322,944 were entitled to the *2d* a pint allowance.

Irrespective of the latest government proposals, it was generally realised that milk rationing would be inevitable. After a further eight months Lord Woolton announced in April 1941 that, although there was still a sufficient supply of milk for the time being, surplus stocks were being converted into condensed milk and cheese in readiness for the winter. As a precautionary measure, dairymen's supplies were cut by 15 per cent and they were instructed to serve customers on a needs basis. (In November milkmen were allowed one tin of condensed milk per customer each month.)

In August 1941 the inevitable decision was taken and it was announced that milk rationing would come into force on 1 October. With the continuation in the postwar years of rationing, in 1948 the allowance per person was still limited to three pints a week.

At the end of the first year of the war legislation was pushed through by the Ministry of Food that with effect from Monday 12 August 1940 it would be an offence to wilfully waste food. The offences created carried stiff penalties – on summary conviction, £100 fine or three months' imprisonment; on indictment, £500 or two years.

The regulations stated that an offence was committed:

1. Where food fit for human consumption is wilfully or negligently damaged or thrown away.
2. Where anyone having custody or control of food fails to take reasonable precautions for its preservation.
3. Where anyone procures a larger quantity than is reasonably required for his purpose and becomes unfit for use.
4. Where anyone [having responsibility for the disposal of food] unreasonably retains it until it becomes unfit for use. (Under this last, shopkeepers who have food and cannot sell it at a reasonable price are exempted.)

Regulations also applied to the sale and supply of food by restaurants, cafés and hotels. Avoidance of the rationing restrictions was not simply a matter of eating out. When dining in a restaurant, customers had to first produce their ration book for the proprietor to take the necessary coupons.

From 10 March 1941, under the Food (Restrictions of Meals in Establishments) Order, it was illegal to obtain a meal in a café or restaurant which contained more than one course of fish, meat, game, poultry, eggs or cheese. The order went on to explain that it did not apply to mixtures of meat such as bacon and sausage, bacon and kidney or veal and ham. However, no combination of poultry and meat, or poultry and bacon was permitted. Additionally, one egg and a portion of bacon, where served together, constituted a meal. In any subsequent prosecution, both the caterer and the customer were equally liable.

The legislation made it practically impossible for food establishments to function. Their main supplier – the butcher – was himself constantly under siege. His first responsibility was to ensure that the housewives registered with him received their due ration; only then could he look towards supplying other customers. Items such as liver, kidneys and hearts, popular substitutes for rationed meats, were themselves soon put on ration. Sausage meat was in short supply and bacon almost non-existent.

To exacerbate the situation in cafés and restaurants, in May 1942 a newly introduced Meals Restriction Order added further constraints to a menu by declaring that while any one course may contain only meat, fish or poultry, additionally, that ingredient must not exceed 25 per cent of the whole. At the same time a maximum charge of 5s for a three-course meal was enforced from 1 June.

The order further required restaurants (other than those specially licensed for use by night workers) to close between the hours of 11 p.m. and 5 a.m. (Many establishments, inhibited by the constraints placed upon them, were already closing in the evening and at weekends.)

An alternative – so far as the public was concerned at least – was a later innovation, the British Restaurant (one opened early in 1944 in Old Milton Street off Bedford Street). These were aimed at providing hot meals at reasonable prices for shop and office workers in the city centre whose workplace did not possess a canteen. Also (as from April 1941) the local authority was permitted to serve food in public air-raid shelters when an alert went on for a long period of time.

In the early summer of 1941, with the heavy bombing of the previous year lending an impetus to the war effort, local schools offered help during the holidays to the overworked Women's Land Army in the district. Wyggeston Girls School and Alderman Newton Boys organised farming camps (this was the second year for the boys' school), while parents from Wyggeston Boys were requested to make their own arrangements with local farmers.

Food prices – driven by ever increasing shortages and a rising cost of living directly associated with rationing – were escalating. In June a 'Food Shop Workers Charter' was agreed by the Retail Food Trades Council, enabling shop workers in the city, who were notoriously underpaid, to achieve some sort of parity with others in a minimum wage agreement. For the purposes of the agreement, shops were divided into two categories: 'A' with takings in excess of £200 per week, and 'B' whose takings were less than that amount.

In group 'A', male managers would be paid 67s to 87s a week, females 55s to 75s; male shop assistants, warehousemen, van salesmen, cashiers and clerks 18s 6d to 62s, females 16s 6d to 40s, all other male workers aged sixteen, 17s 6d.

In group 'B', male managers 65s to 85s a week female 53s to 73s; male shop assistants, warehousemen and so on 16s 6d to 60s, female 14s 6d to 38s; all other male workers, aged sixteen, 15s 6d.

The rates agreed were for a 48-hour week, not including meal breaks, plus a thirty-minute unpaid 'clearing up' period after the shop was shut. The charter also granted managers twelve days paid holiday a year and other staff six days. While the agreement had no material effect on the rationing situation, it did help to make working conditions for those in the beleaguered food industry a little easier.

During the summer of 1941 the patience of many people began to run out with certain shopkeepers and market stallholders obviously attempting to make an excessive profit out of the shortages by either overcharging, or making the purchase of a commodity that was in short supply subject to the customer buying something else at the same time (a practice that was, under the Regulations, illegal).

In July there were ugly scenes in the Market Place as housewives demanded to know why strawberries, the price of which was controlled at 1s 2d per lb, were being sold for 2s 6d a 2lb chip (small box, sometimes referred to as a 'punnet'). Traders blandly explained that they were 'covering their costs' by charging 2d each for the containers. At other stalls the police were summoned over allegations that supplies of the coveted strawberries were being 'put under the counter' for selected customers.

Elsewhere scarcities in the city pushed the price of old potatoes up to 1d per 1lb and that of new potatoes to 3½d. As the summer progressed shortages in the Retail Market (at that time the benchmark for gauging local prices) became more pronounced. Fruit became almost unobtainable; cherries, when available, sold for between 2s and 4s per 1lb. As from the middle of the month the price of tomatoes was fixed at between 1s 2d and 1s 4d per 1lb.

Queues formed outside shops and in front of market stalls when, in the second week of August, an 'off-ration' supply of oranges arrived in the town. It was to be another two years (September 1943) before the Leicestershire and Rutland Allocation Committee announced that a limited supply of oranges was once again available. In the city the Food Control Committee quickly stepped in and imposed a local ration of 1lb of oranges per week (when available) to holders of green (RB 2) children's ration cards. The reason for this measure, it was stated, was to prevent villagers from the county coming into Leicester market and buying up supplies intended for city ration-book holders.

Between 1943 and 1944, with the war progressing towards an Allied victory, supplies of foreign-grown fruit became more readily available, and before Christmas 1943 Col J.J. Llewellin, who had taken over from Lord Woolton as Minister of Food, announced that between January and April the following year supplies of oranges would be arriving from Spain and Palestine. An allowance (which would not be available to the hotel and catering trade) could be expected in each food area at four-weekly intervals. The supplies would not be rationed, but an allocation on the same basis as the existing children's ration should be expected. Instructions were given to retailers that the fruit was to be on display for a five-day period and sales were to be restricted – on the production of a ration book (to prove that the purchaser was registered in that food area) – to 1lb per client. The five-day ruling was based on the premise that after that period of time the product was no longer fresh and could be sold without restriction.

Efforts – often very successful – were made by many of the bigger stores to control sales of non-rationed goods in order to conserve supplies. In September 1941 Joices, 'The Biscuit People', whose premises were at 4 Belvoir Street, made a self-regulating offer to their clients. Dealing initially with existing, regular customers, they offered to issue a voluntary card to those who registered with them, which would guarantee them a supply of 4oz per person of biscuits on a weekly basis. They made the proviso that in future non-registered clients would not be served until all of those who were cardholders had been supplied.

In an era when suburban supermarkets and out-of-town shopping centres are the norm, the provision of items such as biscuits may seem extremely mundane. However, it must be appreciated that during the 1940s and '50s the majority of housewives travelled, usually on a weekly basis by bus or tramcar, into the city centre to make their main weekly purchases.

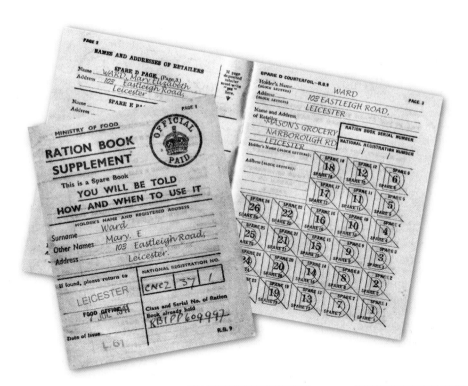

Ration books were issued to the British public for the first time during the Second World War. Unlike the previous war when rationing was not introduced until the last months of the conflict, local authorities, including Leicester City Council, had large stocks of books held in readiness by the end of November 1939. (*Author's Collection*)

One of the first commodities to become subject to restrictions, meat was put on to ration at the beginning of 1940. (*Author's Collection*)

MINISTRY OF FOOD

MEAT RATIONING
begins
ON MONDAY

On and after Monday March 11th, the full meat ration will be 1/10d. worth per week, or 11d. for young children with a Child's Ration Book.

A start will be made with Meat Coupon No. 10 - and coupons Nos. 1 to 9 should therefore be cut out and destroyed. If for any reason you have not Registered - *do so at once.*

No coupons are required for liver, kidney, tripe, heart, ox-tail, etc., or for poultry or game. Sausages, meat pies, and galantines containing not more than 50% meat are not to be rationed at present.

No coupons are required for meat served by Canteens, Schools, Restaurants and Catering establishments - which are all rationed at the sources of supply.

WHEN SHOPPING REMEMBER:

1 During the war our meat supplies are bound to vary from time to time. When you cannot get just what you want in a particular week, be ready to take something else - your butcher will be glad to advise you.

2 When you cannot get Imported Beef, bear in mind that our fighting Forces, whose needs must come first, consume a large proportion of our supplies. Remember that the eating of Home -killed instead of Imported meat saves shipping space and foreign exchange.

RATIONING IS PART OF NATIONAL DEFENCE

AN ANNOUNCEMENT BY THE MINISTRY OF FOOD, GT. WESTMINSTER HOUSE,

This advertisement for Lyons tea from 1943 is an excellent example of the wartime spirit that was generated by advertising. Tea was one of the commodities that remained on coupons for some time after the war, not being de-restricted until February 1952. (*Courtesy of C. Holder, J. Lyons & Co. Ltd*)

Clothing did not escape government attention, and on Monday 2 June 1941 it was announced that with immediate effect clothing coupons were to be brought in. The timing of the move caught both traders and public unawares and led to a good deal of ill feeling. Large stores and market traders alike protested loudly that with the points system, arbitrarily imposed, they would be unable to sell off the large stocks of summer season's goods that they were holding. This was of course what the government intended. Rather than giving retailers a date – probably a month hence – and allowing them to cash in on massive stock clearance sales, they closed the market down and ensured that items would be released to the public slowly.

There was still some degree of panic buying and city centre shops were initially inundated by men and women attempting to use all of their coupons (allocated on a 'points' system) as quickly as possible before stocks of particular items ran low.

After a short while the rush ceased and normal trading was resumed. Adjustments were made from time to time to the points allowances depending on the availability of materials. In June 1942, in a move to conserve the amount of cloth used in men's clothes, the production of double-breasted suits and trousers with turn-ups was banned. In September of that year the Board of Trade also issued an instruction to manufacturers that for the rest of the war, men's socks were to be manufactured five inches shorter in the leg. (In fact, the fashion of men's everyday socks being knee length never returned.) Along with the restrictions on men's wear in the summer of 1942 came the news that the number of clothing points granted to adults would be cut from sixty-six to fifty-one coupons a year. Industrial workers were allowed an extra ten points, and women working in industry were issued with three-piece overalls which could be replaced one item at a time.

A new type of clothing, again based on a national standard (as also happened with shoes), appeared on the market. Made to a budget price from cheap materials and using a minimum amount of cloth, this was entitled 'Utility Clothing', and bore a distinctive government standards mark.

As a final gesture, in May 1942 it was announced by the Board of Trade that 'three million pairs of silk and silk-mix, ladies stockings will be released to shops in Britain during the next few months – after that there will be no more until the end of the war'. Once these supplies were exhausted, many women resorted to subterfuges such as staining their calves with tea or gravy browning and drawing a seam up the back of their legs with eyeliner.

Domestic and commercial supplies of coal were from the outset a prime source of worry for the government, and it is to their credit that for the duration of the war they managed to avoid rationing them. As the second winter of the war approached, with the pre-war stockpiles that had seen the nation through the winter of 1939/40 beginning to dwindle, the government instructed local authorities to appoint officers to be responsible for the unpalatable task of ensuring that fuel was apportioned to consumers fairly. In Leicester, D.R. Stokes of Messrs T. Simpson & Co., together with William Minty from the Leicester Co-operative Society, became the (unpaid) District Household Coal Officers for the city.

There were the ineluctable problems of 'supply and demand – rich versus poor'. A survey of coal merchants in the city soon revealed that during the summer months many of the thrifty and more affluent members of society had ensured that their coal cellars were filled to capacity and would, with a little care and minimal replenishment, be able to see their way through the coming winter. It was those in the poorer districts that were going to experience difficulties. Able only to afford to buy what was needed on a weekly basis, they had not been able to stock up in readiness for the cold weather and were now faced with a bleak winter.

Another problem was that, from the outset, demand exceeded supply. Firstly, even if an adequate amount of coal could be brought into the city, storage would pose a problem and it was too late on in the year for the local authority to think about setting up a central dump. More problematic was the fact that local mines were on short time, many working only four days a week, which meant that Leicester City Council would have to vie with other authorities in bidding for lower-grade coal from either Northumberland or Wales.

For the next sixteen months, by various means, supplies to Leicester householders and businesses were maintained. Often where coal was not available it was possible to substitute coke. In March 1942 the Council had no option but to restrict domestic supplies of coal to 4cwt every three weeks. In June, with a reduction in demand during the summer months, each household in the city was permitted to buy 1 ton of fuel, of which not more than half a ton could be domestic-grade coal, to set aside as a store for the winter. Householders who chose not to purchase the full amount, or could not burn coke or anthracite, were allowed to acquire no more than 10cwt (half a ton) of coal. Once more, those who were – literally – left out in the cold were the people who could not afford to make the one-off purchase.

The entire question of domestic fuel was balanced against industrial needs. The mining industry was working to full capacity trying to meet the ever increasing demands. In October 1942 the Ministry of Fuel reported that for the period June to July the output per week had averaged 3.92 million tons; by the first week in October this had risen to 4.03 million tons.

Throughout 1943 and the ensuing winter things did not improve. Sickness levels, especially in factories and among public transport workers, soared owing to a combination of poor diet and inadequate warmth. During February 1944 the Leicester Fuel Overseer's office dealt with 2,000 hardship applications where increased supplies were permitted. In answer to the inevitable questioning by the public, the Council replied that while coal was not on ration, supplies were limited and could only be distributed on a needs basis. For that month (February), with the winter cold biting deeper each day, the allowance was 5cwt (a quarter of a ton) to each household. Matters were not helped when, with 70,000 miners on strike in the Welsh coalfields, production dropped by 60,000 tons a day.

During the final winter of the war Leicester's coal stocks were at an all-time low owing to further cuts in output, as well as increased transport problems caused by the severe weather that slowed the industry down. There was little that could be done for those queuing outside the Leicester Fuel Office other than to issue permits for extra supplies, which in the absence of any coal in the merchants' yards were of little value.

By the beginning of 1944, although the outcome of the war was not in any doubt, economic constraints could not be eased, and in fact continued so far as rationing was concerned until 1954. In mid-January 1943, with an increase in supplies of home-grown produce to some degree alleviating the situation with regard to vegetables, the sale of certain items such as onions was de-restricted. Meat was declared still to be in extremely short supply and, where possible, fish was to be substituted. With the winter cold affecting people in under-heated workplaces, all firms employing young people (under eighteen years of age) were given the opportunity to secure a supply of 'National Cocoa', as a beverage to be served during working hours. Purchased direct from the manufacturers in 20lb tins, each one contained (it was claimed) sufficient to make 320 drinks. This product was also made available to outdoor workers on farms that included members of the Women's Land Army.

For the sixth and final Christmas of the war (1944) special efforts were made by everyone to make it a successful one. Extra rations, where available, were granted on a temporary basis for the festive period. On 10 December children and youngsters between the age of six months and eighteen years were granted an additional ration of a ½lb of sweets. During the December coupon period housewives received an extra ½lb of butter and ½lb of margarine which brought the margarine allowance up to 16oz.

Additional supplies of dried fruits were released for the production of Christmas puddings and cakes, at 9d per lb and eight ration points. For those who did not want to make their own, Christmas puddings were available in the shops at 2s for the 1lb size and 3s 7d for the larger ones weighing 2lb. The December meat ration was increased from 1s 2d to 1s 10d and was supplemented with the provision of imported turkeys. With convoys now getting through to Britain from the Middle East, 9,000 tons of dates at 3d (and one ration point) for a ¼lb packet appeared on grocers' shelves. A delivery of 22,000 tons of sultanas and 4,000 tons of raisins also arrived at the docks. Leicester Food Committee issued a statement saying that for the fortnight before Christmas the contents of manufactured meat pies and similar goods would be '100 per cent of pre-war as opposed to the usual 60 per cent'. For old-age pensioners (over seventy years of age), an extra ounce of tea a week would be granted on a permanent basis. In a final note of optimism, Col Llewellin (Minister of Food) told the country that his department had secured all the exportable sugar supplies through to the end of August 1946 from Australia, South Africa, the British West Indies, British Guiana, the East African Territories, Fiji and Haiti.

Despite this buoyancy, rationing was not to end with the war. As late as 1948 a typical weekly ration for one person was 7oz of butter and margarine combined, 1s 5d worth of meat, 2oz of tea, 8oz of sugar, 1½oz of cheese, 2oz of cooking fats, and one egg per ration book when available.

Continuing economic hardship and shortages of materials were, in the immediate postwar years, a major problem for every country in Europe – irrespective of which side they had fought on. In April 1947 the American Secretary of State, Gen George C. Marshall, proposed a plan to rescue the economies of the European countries, with resources based in the United States. The plan which he proposed, and which was accepted by Congress, was officially termed 'The European Recovery Plan of 1948'; it became known historically, however, simply as 'The Marshall Plan'. Through a system of economic cooperation, the countries of Western Europe were provided with $13.3 billion worth of aid in a programme which lasted until December 1951.

The motives behind the Marshall Plan were not totally philanthropic. America's own stability and future strategies were based upon a climate of postwar stability in Europe. Economically, once pre-war trading processes had been restored through a healthy

On VE Day the celebrations took little account of the shortages, and parties were held in almost every street and park in the city. *(Courtesy of* Leicester Mercury*)*

import–export system, then America could begin to recover some of the millions of dollars that had been expended on her own war effort. Politically, a revitalised and strong Europe would provide a bulwark against the perceived threat from Communism, with which the Americans were developing a paranoid preoccupation.

At home, in the early postwar years (1946 and 1947) frozen foods began for the first time to appear in shops, and such things as whale meat could be seen for sale for a short time as a substitute for more conventional meat. A serious dock strike in 1948 caused disruption to supplies, when over two hundred ships lay alongside in the ports waiting to be unloaded. Troops were called in to break the strike, and the meat ration was cut for a short while to 6d a week.

Throughout the late 1940s and into the mid-'50s Leicester and the rest of Britain existed in a climate of continuing hardship, with food, fuel and materials in short supply, though American aid eased the situation, the sheer determination of the British people helped them get through the hard times. Gradually, as the passing of each month and year released more commodities from the 'controlled list', the situation eased, until eventually life came back to normal.

First, in May 1947 bread was taken off ration, followed the next year by preserves, and a year later in 1949, clothes. In February 1952 sales of tea were de-restricted, and in 1953 eggs and sugar came back on to the free market. In May 1954 fats were taken off the ration card, and last – and most welcome – in June the sale of meat was de-restricted.

CHAPTER EIGHT

Planning Ahead: 1944

With the beginning of 1944, the knowledge that after five years of war an Allied victory was now only going to be a matter of time gave the people of Leicester a huge impetus to gather their remaining resources and to plan for the future. During the last six months of the previous year the newspapers and BBC broadcasts had kept them informed on a daily basis of the developments abroad. Italy had surrendered to the invading British and American forces, the Russians had retaken the Crimea and Estonia, and, most importantly, the Battle of the Atlantic, undoubtedly the most protracted and unforgiving engagement of the entire war, was virtually over. After June 1943, with an enhanced air and surface escort system for the convoys capable of destroying more and more U-boats, the ships bringing supplies and men across from North America began to arrive in ever increasing numbers.

Although rationing was to continue well into the postwar years, supplies of food and other materials in Leicester began – with the notable exception of coal – to ease. A strike in the coalfields of South Wales in the early part of the year quickly spread. In March 70,000 men, out of a workforce of 100,000, were refusing to work, resulting in a huge drop in output.

The basis of the dispute concerned the role of 'Bevin boys' (named after Ernest Bevin, the Minister for Labour) in the coal mines. From December 1943 until the end of the war, to compensate for a loss to the industry of nearly 40,000 miners who had been taken away from the pits, 10 per cent of male conscripts between the ages of eighteen and twenty-five were sent into the mining industry as opposed to the Armed Services. In all 48,000 young men went to work in the mines of England and Wales. The mining placements were not popular with either the conscripts, many of whom would have preferred to serve in uniform, nor the miners who saw them as unskilled 'black-leg' labour. The current dispute was over the fact that the Bevin boys were earning the same £5 a week basic wage as a skilled haulier or repairer who had spent thirty years in the trade.

The strike had an immediate effect on supplies. Although the formal rationing of coal had been avoided during the winter of 1943/4, supplies were apportioned out at 5cwt (a quarter of a ton) per household. During February the Leicester Fuel Overseer's office dealt with 2,000 cases of hardship which, upon investigation, resulted in extra supplies being allowed. Particular problems arose in premises that were sublet into flats, where it was difficult to make a clear assessment of how much coal should be supplied to individual users. In these instances an engineer was required to visit each applicant and judge what was a fair allowance.

In an effort to improve the canteen facilities for those who worked in the city centre, at the beginning of autumn 1943 a new 'Blitz Kitchen' had been set up off Charles Street at the rear of the Labour Exchange. Manned by a combined team of workers from the WVS, Girls Training Corps and the cooks of the Education Staff, it was capable of providing 1,000 meals a day. Once prepared, the food was delivered in containers to the newly opened British Restaurant in Old Milton Street.

By the middle of the war supplies and munitions were being stored in every available location, including this one at the Ulverscroft Road army depot. *(Courtesy of* Leicester Mercury*)*

(The Labour Exchange had only recently moved to this site before the war. Originally opened in 1910 in Albion Street (near to its junction with Chatham Street) as the 'Board of Trade Labour Exchange', it remained there until the 1930s when sometime between 1932 and 1936 it was relocated to Lee Street.)

It was not only the miners who had grounds to complain about pay and conditions. Sensing that the end of the war was imminent, the teachers' unions began to make their position known.

At the annual Teachers' Conference in Blackpool during the second week in April, representatives from the schools in Leicester added their weight to claims that since 1939 their profession had dropped behind on the pay scales. Along with the rest of the country, Leicester teachers were receiving a war bonus of £1 a week for men and 16s 5d for women. As was pointed out by one delegate, of 200,000 teachers in England and Wales 50,000 were earning less than £5 a week and 30,000 less than £4.

In an attempt to assist the servicemen who were presently returning to the city no longer fit for active duty, the City Council began issuing special business permits. Where an ex-serviceman had previously owned a food shop, it was decided that on his return he would automatically be granted a licence to resume trading, and would be allowed to re-open his business without being subject to any form of restriction. Additionally he would be given a credit of 3,000 ration points in order to enable him to obtain stock. The only provisos were that the person must not have sold his business before going into the Forces, and that trading must begin within four weeks of the licence being granted. In May 1945 the British Legion produced a 'Badge of Services' poster for them to display in their shop windows. The scheme was also extended to those existing traders in the town who had lost their premises through enemy action.

There were also those who, with an eye to the future, had made provision according to the laws of demand and supply. Many motor dealers in the city, whose businesses over recent years had probably suffered more than most, now began to bring out of storage a carefully preserved selection of motor vehicles that, for the first time since petrol rationing was introduced in 1939, were again worth something. Foreseeing an end to the restrictions imposed over the last two years, those with the cash to spare had bought up cheaply and put into store a wide collection of used motor cars and commercial vehicles. Prices suddenly soared. A 10hp car that in 1939 had been worth between £180 and £275 was now on the forecourt at up to £600. In the larger range, 14hp vehicles had risen from £230 to £400.

There were two major subjects for discussion at the beginning of the year. The first was the radical proposals of the soon to be enacted Beveridge Report, which promised that once the war was over every man, woman and child in the country would receive free medical treatment, drugs and medicines. (The estimated cost of the new Health Service was projected to be £148 million a year.) The second was the Education Bill that was to come into force the following year. The fact that it would raise the school-leaving age from fourteen to fifteen – and additionally proposed that at a later date it be raised again to sixteen – posed serious logistical and financial difficulties for the Leicester Education Committee.

Working on the higher figure of sixteen as a school-leaving age meant that a serious increase in education facilities around the city would be called for. Eleven new schools, including a Gateway School for Girls, were required to accommodate the increase in the number of students. An overhaul of the existing schools system indicated that five infant, seven junior, five intermediate and four secondary schools in the city were outdated and would have to be replaced.

Another consequence of raising the age, even to fifteen, meant that a further 3,700 school places would be required. Five senior and intermediate schools would need replacing: Belper Street, King Richard's Road Boys, King Richard's Road Girls, Christ Church and Belgrave Road. On a basis of 480 pupils at each, this would require five post-primary schools for girls and six for boys. It was decided that in post-primary education all schools would be referred to as secondary schools, but of three distinct types – grammar, technical and modern.

Those in the City Council responsible for future planning began to take stock in other areas. For some months the Council had been considering its postwar position. In September 1943, in the knowledge that the blackout restrictions must soon be lifted, £4,235 had been spent on the purchase of electric filaments, gaseous discharge lamps, gas nozzles and reflectors, ready for the day (or night) when full lighting levels were restored. It was, the Finance Committee considered, essential to buy early while stocks were available and not wait until the end of the war when the needs of every other local authority in the country would be driving prices up.

The National Fire Service, now that the danger of water mains being damaged by bombing had passed, began to dismantle its on-street static water tanks (many of which were now the repositories of numerous old bicycles, pram frames and other rubbish) in Charles Street and London Road.

Although Charles Keene in his job as Deputy Regional ARP Commissioner now worked from an office in Nottingham, he still maintained a firm interest in his civic commitments in Leicester, and during January 1944 he accepted the position as Chairman of the Leicester Reconstruction Committee.

The new committee which Keene chaired was formed on the recommendations of Lord Woolton, who having moved on from the Ministry of Food now headed the Ministry of Reconstruction. In line with a national brief, one of the matters that it was directed to examine was the requirement for housing and amenities.

Of prime importance was the fact that there existed in the city centre more land than would be required for industrial purposes. During the preceding twenty years the Council had spent over £3 million on the development of the city centre and now needed to consider the removal of some of the slum districts, such as Wharf Street, that existed on its periphery. (There was also a controversial proposal on the table to develop part of the city into a 'civic centre' – opponents to the idea felt that other cities such as Nottingham and Newcastle that were making plans to take such projects *out* of their city centres had been better advised.) A prime consideration, however, was that if all of the substandard properties built before 1880 were demolished because they were unsuitable for habitation, a need would be created for the building of 46,000 new houses to replace them.

This then led to the further question of where large numbers of new houses could be built, and it was decided to construct a new housing estate on the north-west boundary of the town; it would be called the New Parks housing estate.

Plans were begun for the erection of 1,150 new houses on sites that were already prepared, and a further 1,900 on the remainder of the ground selected for the estate. There was, however, one major problem. The area on which the new housing estate was to be built was already in use by the government – as a War Department tank park. Until the armoured vehicles were removed no work could be started.

A side issue was that the building work – when it started – would encroach on to the golf course at the top of Western Park. Unwilling to take away one of the few public sports amenities to survive the war, the Council gave priority to acquiring the adjoining land.

New houses would be of little use without the services required to make the building projects viable, and it was obvious that a further concern would be the laying down of drainage and sewers, together with adequate road systems, for the proposed development of 2,000 houses on various sites identified by the City Council.

One option available that would give the housing scheme an impetus was the use of prefabricated 'Portal' houses. In a similar manner to the 'Belisha beacon' being named after Leslie Hore-Belisha, the minister responsible for its appearance on pedestrian crossings, and the 'Anderson shelter' being named after the Home Secretary at whose instigation the shelters became a byword for air-raid precautions, the 'Portal house' took its name from the Minister of Works – Lord Portal.

Built from plywood sections and bolted together on to a steel frame in a style similar to that used in America, these chalet-type houses (quickly to be nicknamed 'prefabs') were an ideal short-term solution to the Council's problems. The prefab was a single-storey building, comprising a living room, two bedrooms, a bathroom and a scullery, and because of the nature of its construction very cheap to build. Crucially, part of this cheapness derived from the fact that they were designed, in British weather conditions, to have a lifespan of only ten years. It was hoped that this would give the Council sufficient breathing space in the postwar years to arrange the completion of more permanent structures. While central government was prepared in the short term to carry the cost of providing the houses, erection and maintenance were at the expense of the local authority.

The decision by the Council to use the Portal houses took some time to reach, and it was not until the middle of October 1944 that the Housing Committee finally placed an order with the government for 750 to be delivered the following summer. Owing to the impermanent nature of the prefabs, in a further cost-cutting exercise it was also proposed that only temporary service roads should be laid down for access in the areas where they were sited. In actual fact, the structures proved far more durable than anyone had anticipated and many were still in evidence (often occupied by the original tenants) forty years later.

A number of sites on Corporation-owned land were selected for the erection of the prefabs. On the Braunstone estate 140 were to be put up on Hockley Farm Road, and just over 200 along Hinckley Road East and West. As part of the New Parks estate, 120 would be erected on Aikman Avenue and 141 on the Groby Road side. The Coleman Road estate would have 158 on Wicklow Drive. The smallest number (and first to be completed as a pilot venture) was 31 on Hughendon Drive at Aylestone, within sight of the gasworks.

In all the scheme provided for 793 houses. The capital cost of the land (which the Council already owned) on which they were to be erected was £19,000, the laying of sewers to the sites £24,209 and access roads £56,875. The annual repayment by the local authority to the government for the cost of the dwellings was £23 10s per house, or £18,635 overall. For a total of 793 houses, albeit of a temporary nature, this was a sound business proposition.

Even though the war was going well, the continued fighting was still creating casualties. Wounded and sick men, on convoy trains from Italy and North Africa, were constantly arriving at the Leicester Royal Infirmary and Leicester General Hospitals. After the June landings in Normandy, D-Day casualties were added to the list. On 6 July – one month after the invasion – a hospital train delivered to the Infirmary and General Hospitals 138 men – including some from Leicester – 94 stretcher cases and 44 walking wounded.

Many of those returning to the city during October, some as casualties, others convoyed in by lorry, were men of the 1st Airborne Division who had fought at Arnhem.

Between the middle of 1943 and spring 1944 the Leicestershire Prisoners of War Comforts Fund added another 693 new names to its register. This brought the total number of city and county men known to be in enemy hands to 1,820. Since the capitulation of Italy in September 1943, 622 PoWs had been transferred from camps in Italy to Germany. The Comforts Fund also reported that since it had

Royal Army Ordnance Corps stores were used to distribute everything from clothing to machinery. *(Courtesy of Leicester Mercury)*

started keeping records 24 men had escaped to Switzerland where they were interned, a further 21 had escaped and made their way back to the British lines and 171 were still unaccounted for. (While to all intents countries such as Switzerland, Sweden and Spain remained neutral throughout the war, their sympathies lay distinctly with the Axis powers.)

During the year 1943–4 the Leicestershire Prisoners of War Comforts Fund sent a total of 2,731 parcels to Leicestershire men in PoW camps. These included 12,500 books, 1,600 games and over 27,000 packets of cigarettes and tobacco. Additionally, £3,479 gathered through street collections and flag days was donated by the fund to the Red Cross Society towards food parcels.

After the Normandy landings of June 1944 information and stories of wartime experiences in the occupied territories began to filter back. One such story related to Agnes Stewart, a Leicester woman who had gone to live in France as a nun before the war.

Following the occupation of France in 1940 the Germans established a large internment camp for civilians of Allied nations at Vittel, 186 miles east of Paris. It was found that among the internees were some three hundred nuns from over a hundred denominations, whose nationalities included English, Scots, Irish, Canadian, South African, Australian and New Zealander. Realising the potential of this group of women to assist in the running of the camp, the Germans allowed them to establish a convent at the Continental Hotel in Vittel, with Agnes Stewart, whose religious name was Mother Gonzague de Marie, as Mother Superior.

Under the guidance of Miss Stewart the nuns initially undertook the care of the elderly in the camp (which encompassed most of Vittel), setting up a collective kitchen and preparing food from the rations provided by the Germans and the Red Cross. Next, Agnes Stewart persuaded the camp commandant to arrange facilities in an adjacent hotel, where eighteen trained nursing sisters were able to establish a hospital.

With the entry of America into the war in December 1941, the numbers in the camp were increased considerably by an influx of American nationals (including a large number of Polish-Americans), many of whom brought children with them. This necessitated further negotiations by the Mother Superior with the Germans before she was allowed to open two schools (one for boys and one for girls), teaching children under thirteen. After the Liberation

German prisoners of war marching along Evington Road. *(Courtesy of Leicestershire Records Office)*

Prisoner-of-war camp in Shady Lane, Evington, on the outskirts of Leicester. *(Courtesy of* Leicester Mercury*)*

of France the camp was closed down and the occupants dispersed to their original homes.

In one of the final major fund-raising efforts of the war, 'Salute the Soldier Week' in May set out to raise £3.5 million in order to equip and maintain the Leicestershire Regiment in the field for the following year. Coming on the heels of the massive recent appeal for a similar amount of money to adopt HMS *Renown*, it is incredible that this bid was actually met.

The week was opened on Friday 12 May by Gen Sir Clive Liddell, Colonel-in-Chief of the 'Tigers'. An extensive programme of entertainments was mounted. The military bands of the Leicestershire Regiment, the Royal Army Ordnance Corps, the Royal Army Pay Corps, the Home Guard and the United States Forces band, accompanied by every type of demonstration and entertainment that could be devised, appeared in all of the city's parks and public places.

On Saturday 13 May a military parade headed by two American tanks filled London Road as it headed through the city centre. On Sunday the main event in Abbey Park included military parades and a display of armour and artillery, accompanied by DUKW landing craft. (The initials DUKW were simply a series of manufacturing codes allocated to the 2½-ton amphibious vehicle by its manufacturers, General Motors: 'D' – 1942 (the year of first manufacture), 'U' – amphibious, 'K' – front-wheel drive, 'W' – rear-wheel drive.) The day was marred by an unfortunate mishap when an aircraft, flown by Alfred Lancelot Wykes, head of the Rearsby firm of Auster Aircraft, crashed at the back of Blackbird Road, killing him. (Wykes was an experienced aviator who had flown as a pilot in the Royal Flying Corps.)

Throughout the city over 4,000 posters advertising the appeal were displayed, and as a finale 3,000 men and women, headed by the Royal Army Ordnance Corps, followed by two platoons of Czechoslovak Infantry, a troop of Cromwell tanks and ten armoured scout cars, driven by women of the ATS, headed one of the largest processions seen in the city. They were followed, marching six abreast, by contingents of the Royal Artillery complete with field guns, an anti-aircraft detachment with two 3.7mm and 40mm gun towers, a thousand men of the City Home Guard Battalion and a thousand ATS personnel. The rear was brought up by three Crusader and three Centaur tanks. At the end of the week the target had been achieved and £3.54 million collected.

The year was not without its personal tragedies. On Thursday 18 May, during 'Salute the Soldier Week', just before 2 p.m., Nora Emily Payne was walking back to work along Toller Road from her lunch-break when she was attacked and stabbed with a dagger. She was found dying of stab wounds in Springfield Road.

The deceased, a single woman of thirty-two, worked as a clerk at the offices of the Petroleum Board in Springfield Road (off London Road), and lived with her parents nearby at 7 Lytton Road, in Clarendon Park. Two years previously she had made friends with a painter and decorator by the name of William Alfred Cowle, who while originating in Norwich was at the time lodging in Elm Street. All of the indications are that Nora Payne had befriended Cowle, who was described at his trial as being extremely depressive, in an open and purely platonic manner. Cowle, who had occasionally visited her at home while her parents were there, had put a much deeper interpretation on the relationship, and three days before her death Nora had written to him asking him, to stop bothering her.

Standing in the entrance to the tunnel at Filbert Street Football Ground before a football match between Leicester City and Derby County, in January 1944, the two uniforms of the ATS and the Red Cross are ideally illustrated. While their caps and greatcoats have an identical pattern, the Red Cross women wear a distinctive light-coloured band around their hats. The metal cap badge of the Auxiliary Territorial Service is very clearly displayed by the two ATS women nearest to the tunnel wall. (*Courtesy of* Leicester Mercury)

On the day of the murder Cowle, who obviously knew the woman's routine of going home for lunch, attacked her in Toller Road. Walking away from the scene, he then gave himself up to a patrolling policeman, Constable John Woods, in nearby Kimberley Road. Tried at Nottingham Assizes the following month, Cowle was found guilty of murder and sentenced to death.

Since the beginning of the year troops from the 82nd United States Airborne Division had been stationed in the district around the city and, as part of their training, one of the units used an old clay pit on the north-east outskirts of the town as a weapon-testing and training range.

On Saturday morning, 8 April – the first day of the Easter school holidays – three local schoolboys, Lawrence Mann and Alan Dilks, both aged fourteen, and Eric Orton who was twelve, went out to play football, but changing their minds made their way out to the clay pit. (The two older boys had in fact left school the

Two paratroopers and a glider trooper of the United States Army 82nd Airborne Division, standing in one of Leicester's side streets. (*Courtesy of* Leicester Mercury)

previous day.) At the range they found what they thought was an old shell casing and decided to take it home with them. The 'shell casing' turned out to be an unexploded bazooka round, which had been left half-buried in the ground to await later removal by US Army engineers.

As the boys were carrying the shell along Fairfax Road it exploded, killing Lawrence Mann and injuring both of his friends and three young girls who were nearby.

Later in the year another tragic accident occurred at 2.40 p.m. on Friday 15 September, when a Thunderbolt fighter of the USAAF crashed into a house at 10 Dovedale Road. The occupant of the house, Florence Rudkin who was upstairs on the landing, escaped with leg injuries; however, her 74-year-old home help, Elizabeth Jackson of 32 Myrtle Road, was killed by falling masonry. The plane, which struck the rear and side of the house, broke up, killing the pilot, before cannoning across the road into the back of a second house at 51 Stoughton Road and catching fire. Two female occupants of the house in Stoughton Road received minor injuries, and Albert Hodgkinson, a Water Board Inspector who was working in the road outside, was injured by flying debris.

July 1944 saw a final concerted aerial attack on London by the Germans, not this time by the bombers of Göring's Luftwaffe but by a new and particularly frightening weapon – the 'V' bomb. These flying bombs – which quickly became known to the British public as 'doodlebugs' or 'buzz bombs' – caused immense damage in the capital. The V1, Hitler's '*Vergeltungswaffe*' or 'revenge weapon', was an unmanned monoplane powered by a simple jet engine, carrying a 1,870lb explosive warhead. The V2 (also known as the A4), a rocket bomb with a pre-set guidance system, represented the world's first guided missile and carried a warhead of 2,200lb. With London as the prime target, 8,900 V1s and 1,115 V2s were launched against British cities through the summer of 1944 and into 1945. As a result, a mass evacuation of children, some with their mothers, many unaccompanied, was once more undertaken.

On the afternoon of Friday 7 July 1944, under the Government Evacuation Scheme, the first train containing children arrived in Leicester. Having been met at the railway station they were taken fifty at a time, by City Transport buses, to one of the seventeen reception centres that had been set up in schools such as The Newry and Sir Jonathan North's. There they were medically examined, given a light meal and a package of food sufficient for the next forty-eight hours (this was to allow their host family time to register them for rationing purposes), and their identity papers verified. Unlike previous occasions, provision was made, should the need arise, for billeting to be compulsory. Initially, however, there were plenty of volunteers and the statutory powers were not invoked.

The second train of the afternoon (carrying, incongruously, among other things, a full churn of milk) arrived at the Great Central station at 4 p.m., to be met by a large reception party of police, WVS, welfare workers and ARP Wardens. A squad of Police Auxiliary Messengers, acting as baggage carriers, helped load up the waiting buses. Having been processed through the reception centres, many of the new arrivals were then taken on to Wardens Posts and other locations to await collection. In some cases local parents queued at post offices to gather up their charges.

Throughout the first two weeks of July trainloads of evacuees continued to pour into Leicester on a daily basis, and the Controller of Civil Defence, Charles Worthington, became aware that as goodwill began to run low it would soon be necessary to impose compulsory billeting. The criteria were simple. There was no

A typical scene at the Great Central railway station in June 1944, when women and children, refugees from the flying-bomb attacks on London, flooded into the city. *(Courtesy of Leicester Mercury)*

age limit to the requirement, so whether a householder was thirty or seventy he or she would be forced to find accommodation based on the number of rooms in the house. A house with two living rooms and three bedrooms would, it was declared, house five people including the original occupants.

In eighteen days a total of 170,000 women and children were evacuated from London to other parts of the country. Conversely, because of the disruption to services caused by the flying bombs, a workforce was also being drafted into the capital from the provinces. On 20 July a group of female volunteer telephonists left Leicester to cover telephone exchanges in London where the staff had been depleted as a result of the bombing.

At the end of July Leicester schools had accepted into their classrooms 8,000 evacuee children, 5,600 of whom were not accompanied by a parent. The school holidays were now starting and the Education Committee felt that it was unwise to put this number of children on to the city streets. It was decided that the city schools would close for one week from 3 August, then, during the following three weeks, would open on a rota system from 14 August until 1 September. As this was a voluntary scheme, it was up to the newly appointed foster parents to decide whether or not they sent the children to these extra classes. Because of the high numbers involved, the Bishop of Leicester turned three churches over to be used as extra schools. Forty-nine teachers arrived from the evacuated areas to assist during the third week of July, with a promise of another fifty during the next two weeks. On 1 August children were still arriving at the rate of 100 a day.

Such measures as were possible were taken to help the foster parents. The WVS issued extra clothing from their stores, while the Ministry of Health arranged with the City Council for the provision of camp-beds and extra bedding, crockery, and so on. Leicester shoe traders also offered to undertake the free repair of 1,200 pairs of shoes a week.

By the time that Dr Somerville Hastings, Chairman of the London County Council, visited the city in the first week in September, 30,000 people (some from the original Blitz of 1940) had been evacuated from London to Leicester. In the recent influx, spread over a period of just nine days, 10,000 mothers and children had been found homes in the city.

Soon after this Duncan Sandys, chairman of the committee put together to coordinate work relating to flying bombs, announced that 'the Battle for London' was virtually over, and that any further attacks were expected to be on a low scale. It had been a traumatic few months. Over 10,000 bombs at the rate of around 100 a day had been targeted on the British mainland. Of these, while some ditched in the North Sea 2,300 got through to the London region. Air cover plus the anti-aircraft batteries mounted along the Thames accounted for many of these, but the casualty rates among the civilian population were high. Up to 4 August 4,735 people (4,350 of whom were in the London area) had been killed. On 13 September, in a steady trickle, the evacuees began to leave Leicester for the return journey home.

It was around this time that the city had one of its narrowest (and least publicised) escapes from disaster of the war, which did not come to light until July 1945 when Royal Observer Corps incident reports were released into the public domain.

Leicester formed part of No. 5 Group ROC, which, based at Coventry, was responsible, through an inter-linked network of thirty-five observation posts, for a 4,000-sq.-mile area extending from the Severn Valley to the Wash. In the Leicester sector there were, within 10 miles of the city, observer posts at Rearsby, Shepshed, Markfield, Birstall, Thurlaston, Fleckney and Billesdon, each manned by personnel who were trained in aircraft identification. (In June 1944 thirty-eight members of No. 5 Group travelled with the D-Day forces to Normandy as spotters.)

On 11 September 1944, following a bombing raid on Germany, an American squadron of B17 'Flying Fortresses', having been engaged after the raid by enemy fighters and suffering heavy losses, was making its way back over the East Midlands. The observer post at Uppingham reported to No. 5 Group ROC control room that the crew of one of the Fortresses, which had a starboard engine on fire, had been seen to bale out, and the empty aircraft was flying, at a height of 3,000ft and dropping, on a westerly course towards Leicester. In Leicester the emergency services were put on alert, although there was nothing that could be done to alter the aircraft's course. Minutes later the ROC post at Billesdon reported the bomber flying over them, now at 1,000ft and losing height rapidly. With one minute of flying time left before hitting the city centre, the aircraft crashed into the ground a quarter of a mile from Leicester East aerodrome.

One of the central Civil Defence units, the Air Raid Wardens in Leicester, did sterling work throughout the war in ensuring that every aspect of the city's defences were maintained. *(Courtesy of* Leicester Mercury*)*

The need to divert the energies of the population back into revitalising the infrastructure of the country was becoming more apparent as the year progressed and the government began preparations for a phased stand down of the Civil Defence and other emergency services. As early as March those members of the Civil Defence no longer required in the city were put to work dismantling aeroplane engines and fuselages for use as spare parts. Moved out to local airfields they worked an eight-hour shift, sleeping on site.

At the beginning of October the Chief Regional Fire Officer of the North Midland Region, T.H. Patrick, announced that several hundred men and women in the region, including Leicester, would be released back to the Ministry of Labour for reassignment – which effectively meant demobilisation. In order to achieve a balanced withdrawal of personnel, consideration was given to the skills of each individual, and those whose return to their previous occupation would be of immediate benefit to a particular industry, trade or profession were released first. Total demobilisation, it was made clear, would not be undertaken until after a ceasefire had been signed.

Throughout the war a network of public air-raid shelters was maintained in the city centre by volunteers. Here a group of Shelter Wardens is being met by the Lord Mayor, Elizabeth Fry, in 1942. Charles Worthington, the ARP Controller for the city, is wearing an RAF brevet on his battledress top, indicating that he had seen service in the First World War. *(Courtesy of Leicestershire Records Office)*

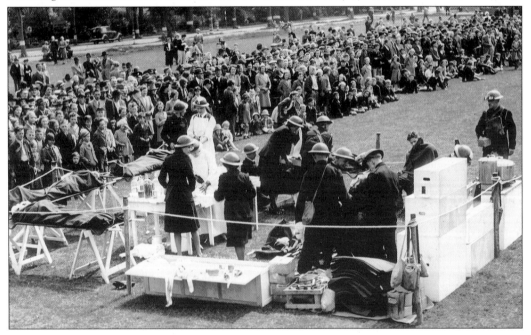

Each summer a variety of displays were provided in the city's parks by the emergency services. These members of the Civil Defence are simulating the conditions to be found in a Casualty Clearing Station. The doctor (wearing a white surgeon's apron) has a white blaze and the letters 'CD' on the front of his helmet. The patient, dressed in a white operating gown, is also incongruously wearing a tin hat. *(Courtesy of Leicestershire Records Office)*

An example of this system is Thomas Bruce Roberts who, having joined the AFS in 1938, was made Divisional Officer, becoming Deputy Commandant in 1940 and Staff Column Officer for No. 9 Fire Force (Leicester) in August 1941. He remained in post until December 1944 when, as a director of T. Roberts & Sons who were local manufacturers, it was apparent that his skills could now be better used in industry and he was released.

At the opposite end of the scale, Divisional Officer Arthur Cramp, who had served as a Regular in the old City Brigade since 1916, was retained as Divisional Officer of the Leicester NFS until September 1945. (During the blitz on Liverpool docks Cramp took a fire-fighting convoy, including sections from Leicester, Nottingham, Derby and Chesterfield, as mutual aid to assist the Liverpool fire-fighters. En route the column was identified and attacked by enemy aircraft, losing two engines. Later, part of his contingent (fifteen pumps and eighty men) was taken by destroyer to Belfast to assist the brigade there.)

In September 1944 it was announced that full-time members of the Home

The danger of poisoned gas attacks, although diminishing as time moved on, was never completely discounted. These two Corporation workers, complete with rubber suits and masks, are about to test the efficacy of a decontaminant. Delivered by stirrup pump, this usually consisted of a strong bleach and water mixture. *(Courtesy of Leicestershire Records Office)*

Guard were to be given notice of discharge and a month's notice as from 15 October. Anyone wishing to return to immediate employment would not be required to serve his notice. On Saturday 2 December a contingent from the city went off to take part in a final review at Hyde Park in London. The same weekend, accompanied by the band of the 1st Leicester Battalion Home Guard, led by their bandmaster, C.A. Anderson, 5,000 members of the Leicester Home Guard paraded for the last time in Victoria Park. (Following the stand down of the Home Guard, Anderson, taking the rank of Inspector, became the bandmaster for the newly formed City Police, Special Constabulary Band.)

CHAPTER NINE

Women's Role

For the second time in twenty-five years, between 1939 and 1945, the role of women in society was altered – this time permanently. During the First World War they departed for the first time from their role as housewives and domestic servants to take the places of men in shops and banks, to work as 'clippies' on the buses and tramcars, and to turn out munitions in the factories. Immediately after the armistice of 1918, as men began to return to the workplace, most women, engaged only for the duration of hostilities, returned to their pre-war positions. The re-engagement of female labour in the Second World War was on a slightly different basis. Initially it was seen as a natural progression, using female labour to fill the gaps which were left on the shop-floor by men going into the Forces, and later moving on to one where they themselves were conscripted, first into industry and then the Armed Forces.

Some previously defunct organisations were re-formed under new identities; others were created to accommodate the necessities of the time. One of the first to appear in 1934 was the Voluntary Emergency Service (VES), which was formed under the combined aegis of the War Office and the Air Ministry. With a loosely defined role, this was seen as the nucleus of a uniformed female body to be used as an ancillary to the Armed Forces. Following the Czech crisis, on 9 September 1938 the VES was reconstituted, granted a Royal Charter and designated the Auxiliary Territorial Service (ATS). From that time onwards, until the end of the war in 1945, the ATS was to be the principal branch of the women's services. (One of the other branches that came under its control was the First Aid Nursing Yeomanry – FANYs.)

With Austria and Czechoslovakia already annexed into the territories of the German Reich, and England only weeks away from a declaration of war, on Thursday 11 July 1939 the women of the newly formed 1st Leicestershire Company, Auxiliary Territorial Services, left Great Central railway station for training by the King's Own Yorkshire Light Infantry at Strensall in Yorkshire.

Contingents of the ATS were to become a familiar sight in and around Leicester and other cities throughout the remainder of the war. At the beginning of 1943 its members were being trained as balloon operators, and in January they were issued with warm naval 'winter clothing' – teddy bear smocks, seamen's boots and woollen stockings – and trained in the use of anti-aircraft weapons. By September 1943, five years after its inception, ATS girls were serving in a multitude of roles (including overseas NAAFI management), both at home and abroad. One in three of them was operating anti-aircraft batteries, and one in sixteen was serving in the Royal Corps of Signals.

In 1916, during the First World War, the Royal Navy was the first of the Services to initiate a branch for female recruits – the Women's Royal Naval Service (WRNS). Membership of the branch, when it was stood down in 1921, numbered 5,000 ratings and 450 officers, serving as cooks, clerks, telegraphers and electricians. A short time after the formation of the ATS it was decided by the government to resurrect the Women's Royal Naval Service.

Women examining camouflage netting at one of the local Royal Army Ordnance Corps storage depots, August 1941. *(Courtesy of* Leicester Mercury*)*

As the First World War was drawing to a close in the spring of 1918, the Royal Flying Corps and the Royal Naval Air Service amalgamated to form the Royal Air Force, at which time the Women's Royal Air Force was also created. Over a relatively short period of time 9,000 women were recruited as clerks, fitters, drivers, cooks and storekeepers into the ranks of the WRAF. In April 1920 the Women's Royal Air Force was disbanded, together with many other women's branches of the Forces and voluntary civilian units. Nineteen years later in the summer of 1939, on 28 June, the former Commander of the WRAF, Helen Gwynne-Vaughan, was asked to become the Head of the newly constituted Women's Auxiliary Air Force. The purpose of the WAAF was to allow their male counterparts in the Royal Air Force to be freed up for aircrew and front-line duties. WAAFs served in a variety of ground-based occupations, most famously as fighter and bomber control operators in RAF communications centres.

In 1938 the Dowager Marchioness of Reading was asked by the Home Secretary to establish a women's organisation whose prime objective would be to assist the ARP and other Civil Defence groups. The Women's Voluntary Service (WVS), which she formed, grew swiftly as volunteers flooded to offer their services, and at the end of the year boasted over 300,000 members (this rose over the next five years to

Women sorting out gasmasks at the Returned Stores depot in readiness for repair and recycling. *(Courtesy of* Leicester Mercury*)*

1 million). Having purchased their own uniform, which consisted of a grey-green tweed suit, felt hat and beetroot-coloured jumper, they were initially limited to organising charity events such as bazaars and garden fêtes in aid of the war effort. This role expanded, however, once the war began, and by June 1940 the Leicester organiser – Mrs Simpson – was supplying staff to the ARP and Civil Defence to assist at the reception centres for the homeless in the city. Furthermore, when the national campaign for scrap metal to be collected for the construction of aeroplanes and tanks got under way during the late summer days of the Battle of Britain, it was the WVS and the ARP Wardens in each of the Leicester districts who undertook to organise the collections. As the war years progressed the role of the WVS broadened to encompass almost every field of activity in which they could be involved. Rest centres and field kitchens for those made homeless by the bombing, along with canteens on railway stations for service personnel travelling around the country or returning from leave, were all staffed by WVS personnel. Many helped out with domestic work in the severely understaffed hospitals, others were employed in checking gasmasks and respirators at distribution centres. When conscription of females came into force during the later years of the war, many of those who were exempted from call-up into either the Armed Forces or industry, because of age or domestic reasons, elected to work for the Women's Voluntary Service.

When France fell in 1940 it became very apparent that a long-term evaluation of Britain's ability to maintain the war effort was needed. A few months later

Sir William Beveridge submitted a report to the Prime Minister that in order to prosecute the war with any hope of success, the Armed Forces and the Home Defence organisations would have to call upon almost 2 million more men and 90,000 women. The circle of supply and need, which had caused so many problems during the previous war, was once again being drawn. There were an estimated 500,000 men immediately available in the labour pool; thereafter, by redrawing the guidelines for male conscription, further numbers could conceivably be found. (The only means by which this could be achieved was through what became known as 'the combing-out process'. Upper and lower age limits for exemptions were narrowed while, at the same time, occupations that had previously been considered to be 'on the reserved list', were reduced. The effectiveness of the system was that it could be repeated on several occasions over a period of time to supply more and more men for the Armed Forces. The trade-off was that each draft further weakened the industrial structure of the country.)

One obvious way in which the shortfall in manpower could be compensated for was by the employment of women. An initial advertising campaign met with limited success. In truth, most women felt that they were already fully occupied

ATS motorcyclist in Town Hall Square. Formed from the Voluntary Emergency Service in September 1938, the Auxiliary Territorial Service became the largest of the women's branches of the Armed Forces. (*Courtesy of* Leicester Mercury)

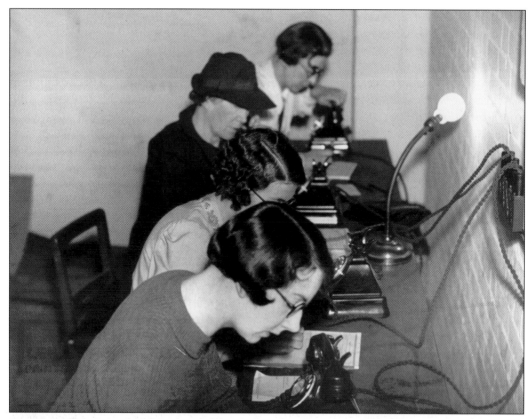

One of the first areas of work undertaken by women was the manning of emergency control room telephones. *(Courtesy of Leicestershire Records Office)*

with managing homes and bringing up families as single parents while their husbands were away fighting. Additionally, most were giving what little spare time they had available to membership of one or another of the Civil Defence sections, working as Fire Guards or helping out in the WVS.

By February 1941 the labour situation was becoming critical, and Leicester women working in the hosiery trade at Corah's 'Wolsey Works', together with girls from the Two Steeples shoe factory in Wigston, were the first to begin three-week training courses as machine operatives in order to relocate to munitions factories in the city. As an added recruiting incentive the local authority set up day nurseries for women to leave their children while they were working. The trickle of volunteers was insufficient to solve the problem and a month later, in March, the Registration of Employment Act required all adults (male and female), who were not liable for military service, to register in anticipation of being directed into various areas of work.

On 19 March 1941 the *Leicester Mercury* announced that the Minister of Labour, Ernest Bevin, was putting in hand moves to call up women of twenty-two and twenty-three into industry. Three weeks later J.M. Lowry, the Chief Labour Supply Officer for the Leicester area, held a meeting with representatives of the Labour Advisory Committee for the boot and shoe trade in the city to discuss how this move could best be implemented. A decision was reached that it was going to be necessary to direct 10 per cent of female labour (around 800 women, who were employed in the shoe factories in administrative, office and manufacturing positions) into munitions work.

The committee was pleasantly surprised to discover that so far as Leicester was concerned, by the end of the next month 400 women – half its target figure – had voluntarily exchanged their positions and moved across into the munitions industries without compulsion.

The weekend of 19–20 April, which was the date set for registration in the city, was a busy one. On Saturday 3,000 girls and women signed on at the Labour Exchange for direction into war work. Among the occupations to which younger women were assigned was the Women's Land Army, and a group of Leicester girls, having registered for work, was duly sent off for training on 22 April to the Midlands Agricultural College at Sutton Bonington.

The Women's Land Army was another of the First World War organisations that was resurrected after 1939. Between 1914 and 1918 over a quarter of a million women worked on the land as agricultural labourers, and the government realised that in this present conflict they had on hand a huge pool of female labour that could be once more mobilised. Before 1939 Britain was importing approximately 60 per cent of its food. Once the sources of these imports were either closed down

Women making binoculars at the firm of Taylor, Taylor and Hobson in January 1941. *(Courtesy of Leicester Mercury)*

by German occupation or impeded by U-boat activity, it became obvious that production on the land would have to be increased. Consequently, by utilising every piece of available ground – pastures, marsh, scrubland and so on – the amount available for cultivation was increased by almost 50 per cent. The Land Army was started early in the Second World War by Lady Denman, and by 1943 90,000 young women over the age of eighteen, commonly known as 'Land Girls', were being employed on farms throughout the country.

As summer approached in 1941 the age limit was lowered to include those of twenty and twenty-one years of age – the '1919 class' – and on 5 May it was announced that 2,500 Leicester girls, having registered the previous Saturday, would now be interviewed at the Labour Exchange for placements in work of national importance. The criterion for further opening up the pool of available female labour was that the age grouping process should move in exactly the opposite direction to that applied to men being conscripted for the Services. Thus in the latter case the age limits were reduced, in the former they were raised. Each time there was a new comb-out of female labour, the qualifying age was increased, consequently the numbers in the catchment group became higher.

On 29 May 1941 women born in 1918 were instructed by the Ministry of Labour and National Service to register by 14 June. At the end of June the net was widened

Postal workers in winter uniform during March 1944. *(Courtesy of* Leicester Mercury)

A Post Office van driver collecting mail in the
city centre. Since the lights are blacked out, the
mudguards and leaf springs have been painted
white for the safety of pedestrians. *(Courtesy of
Leicester Mercury)*

to take in women of twenty-three and
twenty-four who were born in 1917.
Many in this class were already working
full time and presented themselves at the
Labour Exchange wearing the uniforms
of post office workers and tramways
conductresses. Some of those who were
not in work which was considered to be
of national importance found themselves drafted into the previously male
domain of the Home Guard as nurses.
There were of necessity exemptions
(from work allocation, not necessarily
from registration), such as pregnant
women, nursing mothers and those with
children of school age.

Another area in which women replaced men. The
Leicester Corporation Electricity Department
began employing women meter readers in June
1942. *(Courtesy of Leicester Mercury)*

Apart from the three men in the picture, all the workforce on the shop-floor at the Partridge Wilson factory are women. *(Courtesy of* Leicester Mercury*)*

Late in July 1941 shopkeepers in the city, alarmed at the rapidity with which female assistants – engaged to replace young men now serving in the Forces – were being redirected away from their workplace into the factories, began to complain bitterly. E.H. Bosworth, the Chairman of the Leicester Chamber of Commerce, took the matter up with the Ministry of Labour who assured him that women of twenty-five and over in the retail trade were in a reserved occupation. It was further explained that where a woman was called for interview at the Labour Exchange, she was given ample opportunity to state her case; if she was transferred to other work, a National Work Notice (issued under the General Defence Regulations) was served, and a letter was sent to her current employer. On receipt of the notice, the subject was then at liberty to lodge an appeal.

One such appeal was made against a notice by Florence Morland, a 22-year-old hosiery overlocker, who refused to replace a male employee as a storekeeper. Losing the appeal she still persisted in her refusal and was fined £2 at the Town Hall Magistrates Court for failing to comply with the notice.

The adjustments to the age scales became almost a monthly occurrence: as from 2 August 1941 women born between 1916 and 1918 were required to register; at the end of the same month, those in the 1915 class were included; in November it was the turn of those whose birthday occurred in 1912, extending registration to thirty-year-olds.

Work of national importance now expanded into almost all areas of production and a diversity of service industries. Female street cleaners were seen in overalls and cap, pushing handcarts through the Leicester streets, or working as station and carriage cleaners at one or other of the railway stations, some trained as canteen cooks, others became telephone operators, crewed buses and tramcars or emptied postboxes. Women also began to appear in the ranks of the ARP and NFS where, among other things, they worked for the Fire Service as motorcycle dispatch riders. (In Leicester, although they did maintenance work on the fire appliances, women did not go out on operational duties.) In October 1942

During the war horse transport was used throughout the city as well as in the rural districts. This van girl is getting a London, Midland and Scottish delivery van ready for the road in August 1941. *(Courtesy of* Leicester Mercury*)*

A dispatch rider working on her machine at Lancaster Place fire station. *(Courtesy of* Leicester Mercury*)*

Women were employed on a variety of duties at Lancaster Place fire station. These two are rolling up a hosepipe that has been hanging out to dry. *(Courtesy of* Leicester Mercury*)*

the first woman ticket collector appeared at the LMS railway station on London Road, and two months later the manager of the City Transport Department reported that he was now employing 350 female conductresses on the tramcar services.

With the increasingly fluid state of affairs with regard to the country's female workforce, clubs and institutes began to spring up in the town for newly arrived placements. On 6 July 1944 the 'V Sign Club' for women war workers was officially opened in the Market Place by Lord Rushcliffe, Chairman of the National Service Hostels Association (the club had been up and running since the middle of June, and already had 720 members on its books). The club, which was run by voluntary workers and funded through central government on a Treasury grant, had the usual reading and games room, and a canteen with a capacity to cater for 200 people at any one time. Additionally, there was a laundry and sewing room and two hairdressing salons. The facilities were used primarily by women who were living in rented rooms around the city, and in many cases their yearly subscriptions were paid for them by their employers.

As 1941 drew to a close military service became very much a reality for the younger women. Men between the ages of eighteen and a half and fifty were already being drafted. (There was a proviso that men over forty-one would not, where possible, be posted on active service.) This move gave the Armed Forces an extra 70,000 men during 1942.

With effect from Saturday 10 January 1942 single women aged twenty to thirty were instructed to register for military service, which meant conscription into the ATS. (Later, groups were allowed to opt for the WAAF or WRNS.) Those engaged in essential war work such as munitions, transport services, agriculture, full-time Civil Defence, nursing, and teaching were, after registration, eligible for an exemption certificate. Female Civil Defence workers were warned that they could now be posted away to other towns and cities.

At the same time restrictions on women finding or changing civilian employment were also tightened. Effective from February 1942, those in the twenty to thirty age group were only permitted to obtain work through their local Employment Exchange. Exemptions to this regulation were those disabled through blindness, and women who had a child living at home with them who was of school age (under fourteen). Although certain professions – architects, probation officers, social workers, chemists, nurses, masseurs, radiographers, teachers and midwives – were exempted from this requirement, it still gave the government control over the activities of a further 2 million women nationally.

Anxious not to miss any opportunity, in March 1942 Bevin, declaring the creation of a 'Youth Scheme', instructed that girls between the ages of sixteen and nineteen had to register for training purposes. In practical terms this was a means for the government to secure a snapshot of the forthcoming labour market, and to ensure that registration requirements were complied with when these girls became old enough for national work or the Forces.

At the end of the first week Leicester women in the appropriate age group had received their call-up papers to join the ATS. The letter which dropped through their doors contained a 4s postal order (for expenses) and a rail voucher to the training camp to which they had been assigned. Those who had opted for industry instead of the Armed Forces were directed to report to various Royal Ordnance factories.

In the middle of that summer, between June and August, Herbert Morrison, the Home Secretary, launched yet another bid to gain volunteers for war work. At the end of a three-week campaign a further 1,200 Leicester women had signed up for different organisations including the NFS. Nationwide, Morrison was asking for 100,000 recruits (male and female) to man the 2,000 NFS stations which had been established across the country. A total of 50,000 men were being sought for operational duties, and a similar number of women were needed to take on non-operational work.

Once again this demand was soon reaffirmed by a mandatory instruction. In September 1942 women were included in the compulsory training by the National Fire Service, to serve as Fire Guards for factories and offices where more than thirty people were employed. In Leicester alone this involved an estimated 65,000 women registering, many of whom would then be immediately exempted because of other duties that they were already performing. (On this occasion the registration process was dealt with at forty-two school halls around the city rather than at the Labour Exchange.)

Fire guarding was still an essential Civil Defence function. Although air raids were now less frequent – Leicester city was not attacked again after June 1941 – the risk was still very real, and one which had to be dealt with. As late in the war as summer 1944 flying-bomb attacks were being carried out on mainland Britain, and the last air-raid warning to be sounded in the city was in March 1945. At the end of September 1942 Charles Worthington, the Civil Defence Controller for Leicester, announced that women in the age group twenty to forty-five would be required to register for residential fire-watching duties. This was intended to release male Fire Guards for use in commercial premises. The strength of the fire-watching organisation in Leicester was impressive, numbering 75 Head and Senior Fire Guards and 48,000 personnel divided up into street parties.

The situation with regard to the employment of female labour had very much stabilised by the end of 1943. Every possible adjustment had been made to age groups, and different registration schemes, compulsory work placements and membership of the Armed Forces had combed out every possible candidate to support the war effort. Although the employment of female labour was in many ways a cheaper option than employing males, it was not necessarily without its

In December 1943 these two women, Terry Dowd and Margaret Ellison, had just qualified as Midland Red bus drivers. *(Courtesy of* Leicester Mercury*)*

difficulties. (Until some years after the war it was common practice for employers to pay female staff at a lower rate than males. An important factor was that, owing to domestic and family commitments, women usually had short working careers. Robert (later Sir Robert) Mark, while Chief Constable of Leicester City Police in the postwar years (1957–67), in a report to the Home Office, once famously declared that, in view of the fact that since the first policewoman was employed by the city in the early 1930s, 'not one had served long enough to qualify for a pension', making them a sound financial investment.)

On the morning of Saturday 17 July 1943, following a dispute with the management of the City Transport Service, 300 female conductresses staged a three-hour strike over a shift system that had been imposed on them.

Introduced three weeks previously (and known as the 'Straight Nine Shift'), with the intention of providing extra cover at peak periods such as early morning, lunchtime and evening rush hour, the shift involved staff working a continuous 8 hours 50 minutes, without a break. The weight of this new working practice fell entirely upon the tramcar crews – owing to driving restrictions, bus drivers (and consequently their conductors) were excluded from the Straight Nine because by law they were obliged to be given a break after five and a half hours.

While ill feeling over the newly imposed régime was being expressed by the majority of the drivers and conductors, it was the women on the 6 a.m. tour of duty that morning, joined by their colleagues, who took a stand against it. About a third of the strikers were members of the Transport and General Workers Union, although the local Union Secretary, Cyril Hadley (who in later years became a familiar figure as a City Magistrate), was not at this stage aware that the stoppage was about to take place.

A meeting, hurriedly convened in the staff canteen at the Abbey Park Road depot, was attended by Hadley, where he was confronted by the strikers together with many more off-duty crews (men and women), who had come in to lend support. A heated confrontation ensued before it was agreed that the men and women would continue to work the shift until the following Thursday when a new agreement on working practices was agreed.

The climate of the times regarding the acceptance of women in the workplace is clearly reflected in a (somewhat Churchillian) statement, made after the dispute

As in the previous war, women were quickly drafted in to work on local transport. This group in February 1940 is training to become tramcar conductresses. *(Courtesy of* Leicester Mercury*)*

was resolved, by Councillor James Pentney, Vice-Chairman of Leicester City Transport that 'the job of the Committee is to provide the best service it can in these exceptional times . . . there is nothing gallant, nor is there honour due, to men or women, who, in this vital crisis are prepared to cease work for even a minute. . . . I would like to suggest however that the inexperience of the women employees in trade union matters is one which ought to receive attention . . .'.

CHAPTER TEN

The Final Months: 1945

J anuary 1945 was dark and bitterly cold. Along with heavy falls of snow, the thermometer plunged. The lowest temperature in the city, with 24°F of frost, was recorded on the night of 25/26 January. In London that night Big Ben froze, and the 7 a.m. time signal was given on BBC radio by a series of pips. In common with the previous winter a flu epidemic hit Leicester, seriously affecting tram and bus services, and laying off sick 240 transport workers.

A climax to the weather was reached on Monday 29 January, when a final heavy fall of snow closed many of the county roads with snowdrifts up to 8ft in depth. In the city, during the last week of the month, snow-clearing tramcars and brine tankers worked to keep the tram rails clear – although some bus routes, notably on the east side of town, taking passengers out to Humberstone and Garden City, were discontinued. Snowploughs, together with troops and gangs of Italian workers, laboured to clear the deep drifts from the city streets, and plumbers from the Corporation Water Department were kept busy dealing with over 1,400 burst pipes.

A degree of urgency was lent to the situation as, in the midst of this freeze-up, Robert Foot, Chairman of the Mining Association of Great Britain, met local pit owners at the Grand Hotel to discuss methods of bringing the Leicestershire mines back up to pre-war production levels. Stocks of coal in merchants' yards were at an all-time low, and queues of needy applicants were forming on a daily basis outside Leicester Fuel office. Cuts in production, combined with transport disruptions resulting from the winter weather, were creating a problem nationally, and Leicester was no worse off than other parts of the country. Coal merchants in the city were not receiving the government's promised 1 ton per household, and were no longer in a position to make up the shortfall with coke, which was now being diverted into industrial furnaces.

The previous autumn, with a lifting of the blackout regulations, the Lighting Department had announced that as from 17 September 1944 full street lighting was to be restored. As soon as possible a complete changeover to electric lighting would be undertaken; meanwhile, the existing gas burners would be modified to give an illumination ten times brighter than that of the blackout 'starlight lighting'. The intention was good but the promise short-lived – a hard winter and a continuing lack of fuel meant that it was impossible to return to pre-war levels. In July 1945, with the war in Europe ended, the Ministry of Fuel and Power instructed that after September all street lights across the country must be switched off at midnight. While for the general public this order effectively meant a return to wartime conditions, for the Lighting Department it was not actually an unwelcome decision. As a large proportion of the street lights were still gas, and with a shortage of lamplighters (after the lay-offs at the beginning of the war the majority of the men had found employment elsewhere), the alternative was to leave the lamps burning all day, which was uneconomical.

This unique picture of troops coming ashore at the D-Day Landings was taken by Sgt Jim Mepham of the Army Film and Photographic Unit, who before the war was a staff photographer on the *Leicester Mercury*. He joined the newspaper team in 1933, where he worked until enlisting in the Leicestershire Regiment at the outbreak of war. Owing to his civilian expertise he was soon transferred to the Film Unit. During his army service, as an official photographer, Mepham accompanied Montgomery's 8th Army on its victorious drive from El Alamein to Tripoli before moving on with the front-line units into the Lebanon and Palestine. When this photograph was published in the United States it was described as 'the greatest picture of the war'. *(Courtesy of* Leicester Mercury*)*

Although making it clear that there was to be no lifting of food restrictions in the foreseeable future, the government attempted to alleviate matters elsewhere. A new child allowance was to be brought in as soon as the war was officially over. Serving soldiers would receive for each child 12*s* 6*d* a week, widows 11*s*, and disabled men with families 7*s* 6*d*. It was a hastily prepared measure, and until it was introduced the government could not say how existing allowances would be affected.

At the beginning of February the government launched a scheme for towns and cities, which had recovered from the bombings of 1940, to assist other areas that were continuing to sustain damage. This primarily meant the capital, and Leicester adopted the London district of Fulham, which in the recent flying-bomb attacks had sustained considerable damage. While those who had been bombed out received a grant from the government to replace such utility items as bedding and furniture, this refurbishment was, because of the economic situation, quite basic. Coordinated by the Ministry of Supply, arrangements were made in Leicester for wardens and the WVS to collect such things as clothing, extra bedding and pots and pans. These were sent to storage depots in Fulham for distribution.

The removal of the anti-blast wall from the front of the Municipal Buildings in Charles Street, 12 May 1945. *(Courtesy of* Leicester Mercury)

Work on the provision of housing remained one of the Council's prime objectives. At the beginning of the year the Housing Committee (already processing 6,500 applications) was informed that the first 160 'Phoenix' models of its Portal houses would be ready for delivery in the early spring. (The original request was for the 'Arcon' model, but this was still in a prototype form and would not be ready in time for building work to begin.)

Part of the new construction plan was – not unexpectedly – that the costs would have to be borne by the ratepayers. In the ten-year period since 1935 increases in Leicester Council's expenditure had risen dramatically: education by 64 per cent, health care 83 per cent, housing 87 per cent, museums and libraries 51 per cent, parks 43 per cent and mental health care by 75 per cent. The new temporary housing scheme would add an extra £11,500 to next year's budget. The inevitable solution was that the city rate would have to be increased by 1s in the pound, to 16s 2d.

Work began in early April 1945 on the first twenty-eight 'prefabs' in Hughendon Drive (one of the initial debates was whether or not the houses should be powered by electricity or gas. The final decision was that the main power supply would be electricity). These were followed by a further hundred on Hockley Farm Road. Allocation of the houses was based on a strict five-point system. First to be accommodated would be disabled ex-servicemen with families, followed in order by men still serving in the Forces, men recently demobilised from the Forces, widows of ex-servicemen with families, and finally other applicants with families who were presently living in rooms. Easy and quick to erect, the first houses were ready for occupation at the end of the second week in June.

Meanwhile, work on housing of a more permanent nature was not being neglected. Under pressure from the local authority, the War Office agreed to the clearance of the armoured vehicle park on the site of the New Parks estate, no later than October. Consequently, plans were provisionally made for building work to begin by the middle of August 1945. (The last tank – a Crusader – was removed from the site on Thursday 27 September.) The new estate was to be primarily (80 per cent) non-parlour, three-bedroom houses. These would be augmented by some two-storey flats and a series of Duplex houses, which in the early days would accommodate two families.

In preparation for the building work to begin, during the summer months 100 German prisoners of war from Scraptoft Camp were taken out daily to the site in lorries. Split into squads of twenty-five working under the supervision of armed guards, they began the digging out of storm drains and other services. Some controversy arose around this time concerning German PoWs. In March 1945 local residents in Evington Lane and Stoughton Drive complained about the close proximity to their gardens to a PoW camp, which was being built on the site of a recently vacated US military camp. The position was exacerbated in April by the escape from the Scraptoft Camp of two prisoners who were later caught on a nearby farm, hiding in a hayrick. New Parks was not the only site where PoW labour was used. During August 1945 another working party of fifty men was sent to remove tram rails from the junction of Clarendon Park Road and Welford Road for relaying at Humberstone. (Plans were being made to discontinue the tramways service as from 1948, in favour of buses.)

In order to conserve existing supplies of materials, in May the government brought into force an order prohibiting the carrying out of any private building work in excess of £10 without the prior grant of a licence. Additionally, even where a licence was granted a limit of £2 a month was placed on the value of work carried out. This created an impossible situation for the building trade, which now found itself almost totally channelled into working on mainstream local authority projects. It was obvious that there had to be a degree of latitude in such a system, and special exemptions were made for the carrying out of emergency repairs such as burst pipes and so on. Home repairs of a do-it-yourself nature were also permitted provided the householders did the work personally for their own benefit.

Houses in the city that had been de-requisitioned by the army were, it was decided, too large for single families and should be turned over to the City Council on a temporary basis for multi-family occupation – by now Leicester had a waiting list of between 7,000 and 8,000 housing applicants. A lengthy legal process was entailed and powers for this course of action were not ratified until August 1945. A month later Leicester Housing Authority took over its first two houses on Sparkenhoe Street that had previously been used for billeting evacuees.

One of the projects being undertaken by Leicester city was the conversion of the now redundant Civil Defence Depots, which had been built after 1940. It was decided that the depots at Humberstone, Western Park and Wigston Lane would be converted for use as schools. Prefabricated buildings were to be erected at Harrison Road, Bridge Road, Moat Road and Melbourne Road Schools. The pupils from King Richard's Road School were transferred to the Civil Defence Depot on Western Park, making the existing buildings available for the girls who were presently housed at Mantle Road School.

The new Education Act caused a substantial increase in the Leicester Education Committee's spending requirements. The committee's budget application for 1944–5, at £580,385, was £76,528 more than the previous year. Of this increase, 80 per cent (£68,885) was directly attributable to the provisions of the new act.

Additionally, the recently implemented Burnham Report on teachers' pay resulted in an application by the Education Committee for £659,020, an increase for the year of £141,515. This amount, as was pointed out by the Director of Education, was based on the existing number of teachers in the city – it did not take account of the projected staff increases that would be required to implement the new legislation which raised the school-leaving age.

In real terms, under the Education Act the local authority would also lose the income previously derived from charging fees in maintained schools, which would incur a cost to the rates of £15,125. Additionally, the committee accepted a further resolution that in future they would not charge fees to students who remained in full- or part-time studies up to the age of nineteen at the Colleges of Art and Technology. Similar concessions were made to those leaving school and undertaking classes at evening institutes.

Industry in general was preparing for the transition back to peacetime working levels. At the beginning of January talks began between the Chamber of Commerce and government as to the best way to achieve this changeover.

It was decided that a national system under the auspices of regional controllers would be the most effective. (While small traders might not be directly affected, large companies and organisations were going to encounter problems. Such things as the decommissioning of 'concentration of contract work', with the lesser firms needing to begin working again and in need of government help with funding; the relocation of men and women into various industries as they were being released from the Forces – all needed to be addressed in a structured manner.)

Leicester would fall within the Board of Trade, North Midlands Region, the appointed controller of which was J.I. Piggott. Responsible directly to Westminster, controllers were appointed in Bristol, Cardiff, Birmingham, Cambridge, Nottingham, Manchester, Leeds, Newcastle upon Tyne and Glasgow.

Regional offices were to have four main functions:

1. Reconversion of industry generally, and the engineering industry in particular, back to peacetime working practices.
2. De-requisitioning of factory and storage space, and the allocation of surplus government factories.
3. Distribution of factory functions as outlined in the Government White Paper on Employment Policy, together with surveys and information [gathering] generally.
4. De-concentration of civilian industries, [and the] release of raw materials and labour (as soon as war needs permit) for civilian production and employment.

As a city whose economy was closely tied to light industries such as hosiery, boot and shoe manufacture and engineering, a smooth transition for Leicester in the postwar period was essential.

It was estimated in March 1945 that around 40,000 men and women would be returning to Leicester from the Armed Forces, and with that in mind a £25,000 Appeal was set up by the Lord Mayor, John Minto, for a British Legion Headquarters to be established. (Although they were ostensibly part of the military, members of the Home Guard did not qualify for membership of the British Legion.) Also, an Advice Centre was provided to help those wishing to set up small businesses.

Demobilised personnel received war gratuities to help them over the initial period of unemployment on their return to civilian life. (At the end of the First World War, this interim stage was covered by an insurance policy issued to every discharged non-commissioned soldier. However, this insurance was not extended to officers –

Officers of the 53rd Field Regiment Royal Artillery who fought in the desert and Italian campaigns, 6 July 1945. Seated in the centre of the front row are Lord Mayor (John Minto) and his wife the Lady Mayoress; between them is Col J.A.S. Hopkins. *(Courtesy of Leicester Mercury)*

based upon a supposition that officers were gentlemen with private incomes. Whether a genuine misconception or a deliberate cost-cutting ploy, this latter exception ignored the fact that for the first time in history a large number of officers were working men who had been promoted in the field, and resulted in much hardship.) A gratuity equivalent to 75 per cent of this allowance was also paid to members of the Civil Defence where the person concerned had been in receipt of a Services-related wage. The requirement demanded that the person must have served full time since 3 September 1939 for more than six months in the Civil Defence, Local Authority Fire Guards, Auxiliary Police, AFS, NFS (other than as a full-time Regular Fireman), or have been a member of the Royal Observer Corps. The gratuity was worked out at a rate of – for men – 7s 6d for each completed month of full-time service since the qualifying date, and for women 5s a month for the same period.

At the end of April Leicester Corporation appointed a Reinstatement Officer to deal with the 2,000 Council employees who were expected to return to the workplace within the coming months. There were approximately 1,800 from the main departments and a further 200 police and education staff.

As the summer progressed various groups of men and women began to return to the city. On Friday 22 June the first group of Leicester ATS women arrived at London Road railway station en route to Northampton for demobilisation. In August a contingent of 800 Royal Artillerymen, recently returned from Italy, paraded along Narborough Road after a Thanksgiving Service at Holy Apostles church. It was anticipated that by the end of the year over a million men and women throughout the country would have been released from the Forces.

It was during the Italian Campaign that the first Victoria Cross of the war to be received by a Leicestershire man was awarded to Pte Richard Henry Burton, aged twenty-two, of Melton, while serving in the Duke of Wellington's Regiment (West Riding).

Pte (later Cpl) Burton's citation read that 'on 8 October 1944 at Monte Ceco, in Italy, when an assault was held up, he rushed forward from his platoon, armed with a Thompson sub-machine gun, and attacked a Spandau machine-gun crew, killing three of the enemy. Later he engaged and disposed of two other machine-gun positions allowing his Company to consolidate their position. Afterwards, despite the fact that most of the men in his platoon were either dead or wounded he repelled two counter-attacks, causing the enemy to retire.' In the same engagement, a sergeant who was with Pte Burton was awarded the Distinguished Conduct Medal and three others received the Military Medal. (Born at Melton Mowbray on 29 January 1923, Richard Burton died on 11 July 1993 at Kirriemuir, Scotland.)

From January onwards Leicester men who had been held as prisoners of war (some for as long as five years, since the Norwegian Campaign) began arriving back home. Returning mainly by sea – often on hospital ships – and then by rail, they arrived in twos and threes at the railway stations. Many had been held in camps deep inside enemy territory in Poland and Upper Silesia (Stalag 344). Twenty Leicester men were among those released from Stalag 9C when Allied troops overran the camp at Mulhausen.

By the end of June, of an estimated 2,203 Leicestershire PoWs held by the Germans, 1,588 had returned home, leaving 615 unaccounted for. There were, however, still large numbers of men held in Japanese hands in the Far East.

In common with the ending of the previous war twenty-seven years earlier, the relaxation of restrictions combined with the return of men who had spent the last five years on active service, brought its problems. Minor infractions of wartime regulations, along with petty crime, increased, and with the easy accessibility of firearms – brought back as side-arms and in kitbags as souvenirs – incidents of violence became more prevalent.

Under the first heading, it was mainly shopkeepers and market traders who fell foul of the Regulations, to which they had for so long dutifully adhered. Sady Jacobs, a furrier of Lincoln Street, and Lily Bird, a market trader, were fined £10 each for selling second-hand clothing on Leicester market without coupons. A household cleaning company in Belgrave Gate was fined for selling brushes at prices above the permitted limit. In April the first prosecution under the Location of Retail Businesses Order was taken against Frederick Bailey, a furniture dealer, and Albert Wakeling, a grocer, for carrying on a business selling radio and electrical goods in Checketts Road without a licence.

Oswald Cole, the Chief Constable, reported that crime in the city had escalated by 91.4 per cent during the last quarter of 1944. There had been a spate of thefts from lorries, railway trucks and delivery vans. Burglary and housebreaking were on the increase and forty-three men, charged with various offences, were awaiting trial at the Quarter Sessions.

At 7.30 p.m. on Thursday 16 November 1944, two men wearing army battledress held up the cashier at the Savoy Cinema with a revolver and made off with £4 17s. The following evening they held up the pay kiosk at the Floral Hall further along the road in Belgrave Gate. On this occasion they fled empty-handed. Later the same night one of the men, John William Warren, a 23-year-old paratrooper who had deserted from his unit, was overheard bragging to a female employee in the amusement arcade near the Clock Tower about being one of the robbers. When arrested by the police he readily admitted the offences and confessed to holding up another cinema in Nottingham. Appearing before Leicester City Magistrates in February, Warren (whose accomplice was never identified) was sentenced to six months' imprisonment with hard labour.

Open late at night and with little security, cinemas were particularly vulnerable. On 25 January 1945 for the second time in six months, while cashing up in his office, the assistant manager of the City Cinema in the Market Place was attacked and left unconscious, having been robbed of the night's takings. Over the first weekend of April a safe containing £5,000 was stolen from the sub-post office in Sanvey Gate by a gang using a lorry. Two nights later, in similar circumstances, a second safe with £400 inside was stolen from the offices of Excel Supply Company in nearby Churchgate.

Just after 1 a.m. on the morning of 4 April Special Constable Kenshall of the LMS Railway Police spotted a man trying car door handles on the car park of the London Road railway station. Suspicious, he questioned the man, Leonard Percival Bennett (thirty-two) of Main Street, Smeeton Westerby. Bennett told the officer that he was waiting for the 5.55 a.m. train to Kibworth, and produced a ticket which was issued in October 1944. Not satisfied, SC Kenshall took him to the police office on the station and contacted Detective Sergeant Huddard who was at the Queen Street depot.

In the police office, Bennett produced an automatic pistol from his coat pocket and said to the Constable, 'Stand back . . . there's eight in this!' Fortunately Kenshall managed to knock the light switch off and escaped from the office, locking the door behind him.

Sergeant Huddard arrived a few minutes later accompanied by PC Arnold of the City Police, whom he had met on his way from the Queen Street depot. Huddard unlocked the office door and went in. For the next 50 minutes he attempted unsuccessfully to talk the man into putting the weapon down. Eventually, offering to return Bennett's identity card (which was on the table between them), Huddard managed to grab the gun, which went off in the ensuing struggle, and disarm him.

Although Bennett was charged with attempted murder, the Court decided that he was unbalanced at the time of the incident, and after spending a few months in prison he was released. He always maintained that he found the automatic pistol, as well as the nine rounds of ammunition in his possession, at Melton market.

This is extremely unlikely, but with the number of firearms in circulation at that time it was not possible to disprove his story.

While there had been a steady trickle of mothers and children leaving Leicester for some months, the official 'all-clear' for evacuees to return to their London homes was not given until the beginning of May. The delay was not unreasonable. Although the threat from flying bombs was now well past, the London authorities needed time to put into place adequate reception facilities for the half a million women and children who had been moved out to safer locations in the provinces. For the Leicester area it was decided that mothers with children would start to return from the end of May, and unaccompanied children from 15 June. To avoid overloading the existing public transport system, special trains were laid on, and coaches dispatched by the London County Council for those returning by road.

The first parties of mothers and children assembled for their departure in local school halls and classrooms ready to be bussed to the LMS station on Monday 4 June, which was a little after the prescribed date. Since the first group of refugees escaping from the flying bombs arrived in Leicester in July 1944 (initially children and then mothers with infants under five), Leicester had accommodated a total of 30,000 evacuees from the London district.

By the end of July 1944, 8,000 evacuee children, 5,600 of whom were not accompanied by a parent, had arrived in Leicester. For many the return journey to London, which began on 15 June 1945 after VE Day, was made in coaches sent by the London County Council. (*Courtesy of* Leicester Mercury)

This artist's impression, which accompanied the fifty-year plan, shows how the centre of Leicester was originally envisaged. It is drawn looking down Horsefair Street, from where it is joined by Pocklington's Walk, towards the existing town hall. In the foreground are the proposed new Municipal Offices, and on the extreme right is part of a complex housing the Law Courts.

It was now time for one of Leicester's most important and imaginative projects of the century – the postwar reconstruction of the city and its road systems – to be moved from the drawing board to the implementation stage.

On the retirement of Arthur Gooseman in February 1941, he was replaced as City Surveyor by John Leslie Beckett. Beckett, who was forty-one years of age when he came to Leicester from Burnley, was engaged at a salary of £1,500 a year. As with so many other cities at the end of the war, Leicester, bomb damaged and short of amenities, was a prime subject for redevelopment and Beckett proved to be equal to the task. In March 1944 he presented the City Council with a fifty-year blueprint for the reconstruction and modernisation of Leicester. Much of what he envisaged came to pass in the ensuing years, while other things proved either to be impractical or, with the passage of time, found to be no longer needed. For instance, one of his main projects involved the creation of a civic centre in the area behind the town hall – an administration centre was later built; it was neither in the location nor the form that Beckett had imagined.

Although many people, including future City Surveyors, worked hard to implement the plan during the next fifty-five years prior to the turn of the century, much of the present aspect of Leicester city and its ring-road system is directly attributable to John Beckett's 1944 blueprint.

The reconstruction plan called for the building of 7,000 new houses on the outskirts, with a civic centre and shopping facilities enclosed by a central ring road within the city itself.

A sports stadium along with a football field capable of seating 75,000 spectators was to be built near to the Aylestone Road section of the River Soar.

At least 6,000 new houses were planned as soon as possible to meet the immediate shortage of working-class accommodation, with a further 2,000 towards the end of the project. (The Council already owned sufficient sites for 7,000.) Beckett pointed out that 3,500 houses would be needed for the

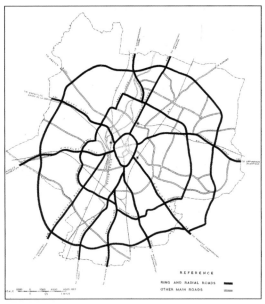

REFERENCE

RING AND RADIAL ROADS

OTHER MAIN ROADS

John Beckett proposed a series of three ring roads, interlinked by the existing main roads leading out of the city.

relocation of tenants made homeless by slum clearance, and that 'there is land in private ownership immediately available for this'. He was doubtless referring here to the Wharf Street area which in the next decade was cleared for replacement by the St Matthews estate.

Still dealing with housing matters, Beckett made detailed plans concerning the laying down of the New Parks estate. A total of 1,050 houses were to be built on ground already prepared, with a further 1,900 spread over the remainder of the area, including that occupied by Western Park Golf Course.

The early creation of three new communities was recommended: New Parks community, with a centre adjacent to Western Park; Braunstone community, with a centre in Braunstone Park; Westcotes community, with a centre on the site of the Westcotes Maternity Home and Wyggeston Hospital. Major roadworks would have to be put in hand for communication and passenger transport to estates such as the New Parks.

Residential areas needed to be insulated from main traffic routes and provision made within such areas for younger children to play and older children to be educated. Each was to have facilities for recreation (such as sports fields), shopping centres and provision for the elderly. Land on the outskirts, presently held for aerodrome purposes, needed to be turned over to modern light industry, while at the same time giving consideration to the future potential of establishing a civil airport.

Probably his most far-sighted design was the laying down of three concentric ring roads in and around the city. The Outer Road would flow around the boundary of the city, from Welford Road (A50 south) clockwise over the A426 at Lutterworth Road, A46 Narborough Road, A47 Hinckley Road, A50 (north) Groby Road, round across the top part of the boundary and down to the main A47 (going out towards Uppingham and the East Coast), before cutting back down again across the A6 (south) London Road.

The Inner Ring Road would run from London Road to Uppingham Road, before swinging across to Melton Road, then joining Abbey Lane, turning back along Henley Road and Fullhurst Avenue. Passing the new prefabricated housing on Hughendon Drive, the line would pass along Knighton Lane to rejoin London Road.

Finally the Central Ring Road provided motorists with a fast route from one side of the city to another without passing through the centre. (It must be borne in mind that, ambitious as these traffic schemes were for the day, neither the City Surveyor nor his contemporaries could have envisaged the increase in traffic flow that the next fifty years would bring.)

John Beckett's comments on this particular route were especially detailed and perceptive:

. . . Oxford Street to the Magazine ([the] archway with surrounding buildings removed will stand as an island to divide traffic). Next island – straight road from West Bridge presents a tree surrounded vista of the Old Guildhall and Cathedral. Next island, point where a curved road from Upper Churchgate goes across to the Great Central Station. Near to the island is suggested a Central Baths site, omnibus station and car park. Next island, Churchgate reaches the Ring Road at this point, south of St Margaret's Church. An extended Churchgate will cross St Margaret's Pasture, skirt Abbey Park and join Abbey Lane near to Grundon Street. Thence the road cuts across old or partially cleared property passing the west end of Christ Church to the crossing of a widened Humberstone Gate near to Nichols Street. On the way down to the island at the junction of Granby Street where Charles Street now emerges, will be a small island marking the spot where it is suggested a road should be taken across the railway to join up with Clipstone Street. The road now completes the circle by skirting the museum grounds and Holy Trinity Church to the island near the Infirmary.

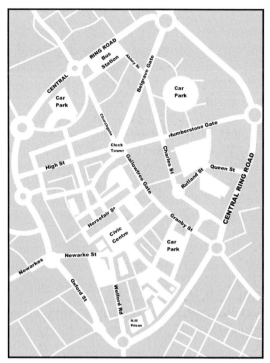

The 1944 city centre and Inner Ring Road scheme as envisaged by John Beckett, Chief Engineer, Surveyor and Planning Officer for Leicester City in his fifty year re-development plan.

Half a century later a detailed study of the present city reveals how much of Beckett's plan came to fruition.

Pivotal to the reconstruction scheme was the creation of a civic centre, which in later years appeared as a multi-storey administrative building in New Walk. The original design, however, was somewhat different. Initially, wrongly placed industry in the centre of the town was to be removed and the area to be zoned into sectors dedicated to administration, business, a cultural headquarters, and centres for shopping, entertainment and hospitality.

The original concept for the 'civic and cultural centre' involved a number of buildings, including law courts, a library, a theatre, and the centralisation of offices for all activities relating to public and national administration. The boundaries of this complex were quite specific: it was to lie in the area enclosed by Granby Street, Belvoir Street, Albion Street, the Central Ring Road, King Street and Marlborough Street.

From original artist's impressions it appears that the demolition of the existing properties back as far as Pocklington's Walk was to remove a substantial number of buildings in this square. An extension of the civic buildings was projected at the far end of the complex fronting up to Horsefair Street. A further proposal was to leave the Market Place and Corn Exchange (with its Rialto Bridge) in their present state, but, in the words of the report, 'in all probability the square will be made into a garden with trees, and will be a high class shopping centre, the existing market probably being moved to the Loseby Lane neighbourhood'.

Not losing sight of the necessity to upgrade the local authority buildings, Beckett made further suggestions. A health centre was needed near to the Leicester Royal Infirmary, and a public swimming bath was to be built on the Central Ring Road, near to St Peter's Lane. The old wholesale fruit and vegetable market was to be demolished and a new bus station erected.

The new bus station was in fact built at the junction of Abbey Street and the Central Ring Road on the site of the old public air-raid shelters, which were converted back to their original usage in December 1944 at a cost of £7,000. Initially known as Burley's Lane bus station, the depot later took the parish name of St Margaret's. In February 1945 the services from its twelve platforms were handling 25,000 people daily. The fact that this station was in operation prior to the reconstruction plan being implemented, and later became the main city bus depot, indicates that the wholesale market proposal was rejected at an early stage – although in later years the Leicester City Transport depot was moved to a site nearby.

In the Southgate Street area, the west front of the cathedral needed to be opened up by knocking down the Alderman Newton's School, and 'consideration given to the future of the district enclosed by Guildhall Lane, Peacock Lane, and Southgate Street'. (A definite visionary, John Beckett seems to have put the march of progress at an absolute premium with scant consideration for the preservation of the past. Southgate Street, the Magazine Barracks, near to The Newarkes, and the lanes backing on to West Bridge, which were among the most historic parts of the city, were all subsequently lost.)

Beckett envisaged the 7½ mile length of the River Soar, as it flowed through the city, being divided into three sections. Along the southern part, from the gasworks at Aylestone to the Outer Ring Road, would be his new 75,000-seater sports stadium, with a smaller ground for a further 15,000 people providing open-air bathing in a championship-sized pool. Also within this area would be a café, children's play park, model yacht pool, sports pavilion, concert hall, gymnasium, library, open-air theatre and a miniature 18-hole golf course. The proposed dimensions were unrealistic and somewhat revealing. With park keepers' lodges on Aylestone Road, and an entrance to the Narborough Road side situated on Meredith Road, it is apparent that he intended the removal of vast numbers of houses and buildings on the south-west side of the city.

For the centre line of the river, from the gasworks to the Castle Gardens and West Bridge, he was content merely to 'beautify the river banks'. Along the northern 2½ miles, there were to be riverside promenades and cycle tracks. Each end (Abbey Park and Thurcaston Road Bridge) would be punctuated by a boating station, café and car park, with a children's boating lake in Abbey Meadows.

It is to John Beckett's credit that while some things took longer to achieve than others, the major part of his project was completed within the given fifty years. In the *Municipal Journal* of September 1956 the Council reported that 'since the war 1,100 houses have been built outside the city boundary at Scraptoft and Eyres Monsell. . . . The Council is in the process of arranging to demolish a thirty acre site [Wharf Street], and will erect 750 dwellings comprising houses, maisonettes, and four storey flats . . . in the ten year period 1945–55, more dwellings have been erected than during the twenty years prior, the annual output is now approximately 1,200 dwellings out of which the Council will make available 600 dwellings yearly for slum clearance re-housing'.

On Wednesday 2 May 1945 the Ministry of Home Security circulated all local authorities in the country with the information that as from 12 noon that day the national air-raid and industrial alarm system would be discontinued. No longer would it be necessary to man post office switchboards on a 24-hour basis for the reception of air-raid initiation messages. Likewise, the Control of Noise Orders prohibiting the sounding of sirens, hooters, rattles and other such instruments, other than to proclaim the imminence of an air raid, were rescinded.

VE Day, Victory in Europe, came on Tuesday 8 May 1945, when at 3 p.m. the Prime Minister, Winston Churchill, announced that the war in Europe would end at 12.01 a.m. Flags, held in readiness in offices and factories, were quickly draped from first-floor windows, and Granby Street, Gallowtree Gate and the Town Hall Square were filled within minutes by a multitude of people.

Careful plans had been laid by the City Council for the forthcoming celebrations. After the declaration post offices were to remain open for one hour before closing, post boxes would be emptied and then there would be no more deliveries that day; a two-day public holiday with pay was proclaimed for all factories in the city.

All retail outlets could close immediately, tobacconists and food shops (other than butchers, who for some reason were given the full holiday) were instructed to remain open for three hours after the declaration, then close for the remainder of the holiday. Milk deliveries remained as normal. Other than where meals were in the process of being served, schools were to close immediately and the children be sent home. Local papers such as the *Leicester Mercury* would not publish an edition on VE Day.

By 10 a.m. on 8 May, in anticipation of the Prime Minister's announcement, large crowds singing 'Rule Britannia' to the strains of the Salvation Army Band gathered in Town Hall Square, which was decked out in fairy lights and flags, including the Red and White Ensigns and Colours of the Royal Air Force. It was the biggest gathering since the declaration of the Armistice in November 1918. A morning Service of Thanksgiving, and a speech by the Lord Mayor, John Minto, were interrupted by a heavy thunderstorm, but few of those gathered left their places. In the Market Place people took shelter from the rain under the awnings of stalls, singing patriotic songs until the weather brightened. (The weather had been particularly unseasonable for the time of year. Over the previous weekend, on Friday night and Saturday morning, a freak snowstorm deposited a blanket over the county. In Hinckley it was followed by rain, hail and lightning. During the night and early morning, 2in of snow settled in Loughborough. Leicester city did marginally better, receiving a fall of only 1in.)

Crowds converged in the Town Hall Square to hear the reading by the Lord Mayor, John Minto, of the official declaration on 8 May 1945 that the war had ended. Many of those gathered had put up umbrellas against the rain that interrupted the proceedings. (*Courtesy of* Leicester Mercury)

As the day progressed the festive spirit took hold of the entire city. Many of those who had remained in Town Hall Square to listen to a speech by the King, broadcast over loudspeakers, remained to dance to music provided by the Special Constabulary Band. At dusk the area was flooded with coloured lights rigged up by men of the City Lighting Department. Businesses and shops, for the first time in five years, left their lights switched on to illuminate the streets. Pub landlords, many ignoring the 'one hour' extension that they had been granted, served out home-made 'Victory Cake' to their customers.

Parties and dancing filled the parks and streets. In a celebration at Hillcrest Workhouse, on Sparkenhoe Street, the cooks baked their own '2-cwt Victory Cake' for the inmates. In Victoria Park one enterprising local was selling 'American Hot Dogs', cooked in the headlight of an army motorcycle, pulled up on its stand with the engine running.

A conga-line dancing around the Clock Tower during the early part of VE Day. The Constable in the centre of the picture is PC 70 Percy Moss. *(Courtesy of* Leicester Mercury*)*

Everywhere, adults and children alike celebrated the ending of the war. *(Courtesy of* Leicester Mercury*)*

In streets all around the suburbs effigies of Hitler were being burned on bonfires blazing away in the middle of the road. Thousands congregated around the Clock Tower, singing and, led by a kilted piper, dancing twelve abreast along Gallowtree Gate. There was one notable absence during the two days of celebrations. Under orders from the American military all US Servicemen in the district were confined to their camps. For the later VJ Day celebrations, however, this restriction was lifted, and an American band on the back of an army lorry provided music for the crowds to dance to in the city centre.

Although the conflict in the Far East was still to be resolved, so far as the British public was concerned the war was effectively over. There remained, however, one further matter to be dealt with. A peacetime government needed to be elected. In addition to those people living in the city, 35,000 Leicester men and women who were still away in the Services were given the option to make a written application for a ballot paper or to vote by proxy, and in July a new government was voted in.

The results, locally and nationally, were in many quarters unexpected. The Conservatives suffered severe losses in the polls. Churchill, who had steered the country through the crises on the Home Front, and was by many perceived to be the architect of victory overseas, was no longer Prime Minister. Locally in the

Parties were held in streets all over the country to celebrate VE Day. *(Courtesy of* Leicester Mercury)

A group of ATS girls and young soldiers join the crowds dancing in streets around the Clock Tower. *(Courtesy of* Leicester Mercury)

county, Sir W. Lindsay Everard (MP for Melton since 1924), Sir William Edge (MP for Bosworth since 1927), Ronald Tree (Market Harborough) and Maj Lawrence Kimball (Loughborough) all lost their seats. City Conservatives fared no better. Capt Charles Waterhouse (MP for Leicester South since 1924) was replaced by Flg Off Herbert Bowden (Labour). Col Abraham Montagu Lyons, in Leicester East, lost his seat to Terence Norbert Donovan KC (Labour) and Ernest Harold Pickering, who had held the Leicester West seat for the Liberals, was ousted by Barnett Janner (Labour).

Following the dropping of two atomic bombs on the cities of Hiroshima and Nagasaki in August 1945 and the subsequent surrender of Japan in September the Second World War came to an end. Once more there were parties and celebrations, with dancing in the streets and fireworks being let off. Again the Town Hall Square was decorated with flags and bunting and crowds gathered for the open-air Service of Thanksgiving. However, on this occasion the celebrations were not conducted with quite the intense fervour that had accompanied VE Day. Victory in Europe was what had signalled for the majority of the population in Leicester, as with the rest of the country, that the war was over – although it was with VJ Day that the conflict actually ended.

CHAPTER ELEVEN

Conclusion

In September 1945, with the end of the war in Asia, peace once more returned to the western world, and life in Leicester reverted to a mixture of the normality of the pre-war years combined with an anticipation (as after the previous war) of a brighter future. There were, though, differences between 1945 and the climate which existed after November 1918. Women did not return en masse to domestic work and the kitchen sink. Many remained at their places in the factories (mainly as hosiery and shoe hands), either through financial need or a reluctance to abandon their new-found independence. (There remained, however, for many years an imbalance in the pay structures between men and women. For example, in boot and shoe factories in 1951 for a 45-hour week a man could expect to earn £7 7s, while a woman doing the same job received only £4 14s. By 1959 this had risen to £12 3s for a man, and to £8 1s for a woman.)

Whatever the reasons, in the postwar years of the 1950s and '60s, as a city, Leicester became renowned for its high proportion of female workers. As industry nationally revitalised so the factories of the staple Leicester trades – boot and shoe, light engineering and hosiery – also picked up, and by the 1960s the city was viewed as being one of the most prosperous in the country. A peak was reached in the mid-1960s when, following the opening of the M1 motorway close to the city boundary, another communications link was added to the rail and waterway networks at the centre of which the city was placed. (The use of the inland waterways as a main commercial transport system quickly fell into disuse after the war, and a short-term decline set in during the mid-'70s when a period of recession hit the town's main industries.)

Along with the rest of the country Leicester experienced what came to be described as the 'postwar baby boom'. The last pre-war figures for the city's population came from the 1931 census (the Depression years of the 1930s were not perceived by the government as being ideal for taking regular national surveys), and gave the population of the city as 239,169. The figure for 1951 peaked at 285,061 (census figure). After this it dropped slightly before levelling out in 1958 to 277,700. A sample census in 1966 gave a figure of 279,030, and the full census of 1971 showed that the numbers had climbed back to 284,210. These figures show a steady rise in the population of Leicester in the years immediately following the war, which have to be set against an ever present mortality rate and (more relevantly) the large numbers of people who in the postwar years emigrated to Commonwealth countries such as Canada, Australia and New Zealand.

Figures for the period after 1971 are not representative of the natural population progression, as there now came a period of high immigration into the city of peoples from the Indian subcontinent and, after 1974, from East Africa. (There had been a steady immigration into the city from the Caribbean area throughout the 1940s and '50s, which also continued.)

These members of the Leicester and District branch of the Normandy Veterans Association formed in 1982, display their Colours outside St Philip's Church at Evington. (*Courtesy of* Leicester Mercury)

After the war Charles Keene continued to be a prominent figure in local politics, becoming an Alderman of the city in 1945 and having the 'Charles Keene College of Further Education' named after him. (In addition to his wartime responsibilities, he served as Chairman and Vice-Chairman of the Education Committee between 1938 and 1946.) Continuing with his interest in John Beckett's plans for the redevelopment of Leicester, Alderman Keene became Chairman of the Town Planning Committee which superseded the original Reconstruction Committee, and in 1952 became Chairman of the Slum Clearance and Redevelopment Committee. Awarded the CBE in 1950 (and later the Freedom of the City in 1962), Charles Keene, during his year as Lord Mayor, was chosen to represent the City of Leicester at the Coronation of Her Majesty Queen Elizabeth II at Westminster in June 1953. He died in 1977 at the age of eighty-five and is buried in his home churchyard at Gaulby.

The other prime mover in ensuring the safety of the city throughout the war, Charles Worthington, also continued to find time from his business activities to pursue his political interests (initially elected to the Council as an Independent Member in 1936, he later represented Evington Ward as a Conservative – unlike Keene, who unusually for a businessman at that time stood as a Labour candidate). Serving on a host of committees, he was awarded the CBE in 1943 for his services as the ARP Controller for the city, and in October 1946, as Lord Mayor, received their Majesties King George VI and Queen Elizabeth when they paid a royal visit to Leicester. Charles Worthington, whose shops throughout the

Former members of the US 82nd Airborne Division return to Leicester to celebrate the anniversary of the D-Day landings, 2 June 1989. The 82nd was based in the county in the months leading up to the invasion on 6 June 1944, and comprised three Parachute and one Glider Regiments operating from sites all over the county. On the night of 5 July 1944 they took off for the Normandy beaches from the airfields at Cottesmore near Oakham and Spanhoe near Corby. *(Courtesy of* Leicester Mercury*)*

For many years after the war the anniversary of the 'Battle of Britain' was celebrated in the city with a parade. On this occasion Wg Cdr R.R. Stanford-Tuck is taking the salute as an RAF contingent from Cottesmore air base march by. *(Courtesy of* Leicester Mercury*)*

city bore the legend 'Let Worthington's Feed You', died on 26 April 1970 aged seventy-three.

Changes inevitably occurred to the institutions with which Leicester people had become familiar. The Fire Services Act 1947 disbanded the National Fire Service and returned the power once more to local authorities to establish their own dedicated brigades. Within months the Leicester City Fire Brigade was re-created, and with the dissolution of the National Fire Service system of Regional Fire Forces Errington McKinnell was quickly back as its Chief Officer.

The tramways system was one of the first to fall victim to progress. Having closed the Welford Road service in 1945 by the effective method of taking up the rails and moving them to Humberstone, a programme of closure was imposed almost as soon as the war had ended. The first horse-drawn tramcar, running

Blessing of the Colours of the United States Air Force (Bruntingthorpe), Civil Defence, Royal Air Force Association, and the Seaforth Highlanders, by the Provost of Leicester the Very Reverend R.J.F. Mayston, on 19 September 1960. On the dais are the Lord Mayor, Councillor Dorothy Russell, and the Lady Mayoress, Miss Patricia Russell. *(Courtesy of Leicester Mercury)*

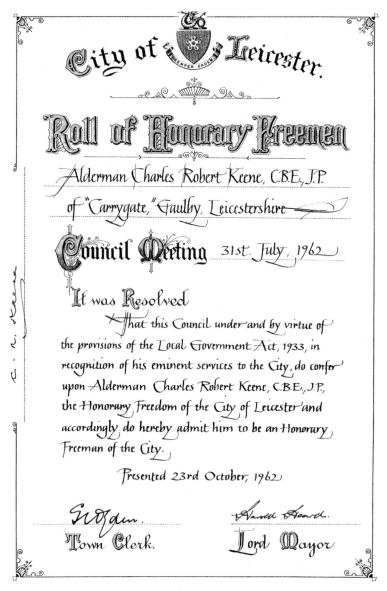

In 1962 Alderman Charles Keene was granted the Freedom of the City of Leicester. *(Courtesy of Leicester City Council)*

from the town centre to Belgrave, made its appearance in 1874; this was followed thirty years later by an electrified system that conveyed passengers from most of the suburbs into the town centre. The last tramcar, which ironically was also one of the first – having been on the rails since the inception of the service – made its final run on 9 November 1948. The old tramways depot was moved in March 1969 from the block which it used to occupy, between Belgrave Gate and Humberstone Gate, to its new location in Rutland Street.

Of the complex rail network that served the city, the stations at Great Central Street and the old 'Great Northern' on Belgrave Road failed to survive government moves in the 1960s to streamline Britain's rail services. The last scheduled train – the 10.10 a.m. Leicester to Skegness – left Great Northern station on Sunday 9 September 1962. Great Central saw its last departure in May 1969.

The Blackbird Road Stadium, which was home to the Leicester Hunters Speedway Team, and in earlier days – as the dog track – scene of the murder of Frank Sykes, survived longer than many others and held its last meeting on 25 October 1985.

Perhaps the most regrettable loss to the city for many was the passing into history of the Leicestershire Regiment, which had started life as the 17th Regiment of Foot. In 1964 the Tigers were absorbed into the Royal Anglian Regiment.

The indisputable fact is that following the war years, with the blueprint provided by John Beckett (who retired in May 1964), Leicester embarked upon a redevelopment that took it into the twenty-first century. Bomb sites were cleared and either built upon or made into open areas, a system of ring roads was created, housing estates were built and slums removed. A civic centre, modern swimming baths and a sports stadium were built. An area around the Clock Tower was demolished and a new Haymarket Shopping Centre created – to be followed later by the adjacent Shires Shopping Centre.

Whatever was achieved during the latter half of the twentieth century is, without doubt, thanks to the efforts of those men and women – some of whom went away to fight the war, others who remained to ensure that there was a place to return to – who dedicated the years between 1939 and 1945 to Wartime Leicester.

Appendix I

Calls attended by Leicester City Fire Brigade during the night of the main bombing raid on Leicester City 19/20 November 1940, taken from the Watch Committee Minutes, November 1940

South Albion Street	St John the Divine Church
Stoughton Street	dwelling house
Aylestone Road	G. Gibbins (printers)
Aylestone Road	Leics City Rugby Football Club
Aylestone Road	cattle market
New Walk	Holy Cross Church
Calais Hill	J.M. Vice (printers)
Upper King Street	dwelling house
Granby Street (nos 101–3)	Victoria Hotel
Granby Street/Charles Street	Midland County Garage
11 Princess Road	dwelling house
Dover Street (no. 42)	A. Kemp Ltd (hosiery factory)
Welford Road (no. 39)	Sandys Ltd (warehouse)
Newarke Street (no. 6)	James Hearth (hosiery factory)
Hughendon Drive	dwelling house
Granby Street (no. 89)	Moore Eady & Murcott Goode (hosiery factory)
King Street (nos 25–31)	Wolsey Ltd (hosiery factory)
Granby Street	Harris Ltd (furnishing store)
Erskine Street	premises not specified
Wharf Street (nos 136–52)	Marvin's Ltd (drapers)
Carley Street	dwelling house
Lead Street	premises not specified
Liverpool Street	dwelling house
Garendon Street	dwelling house
Wharf Street	premises not specified
Abbey lane (no. 234)	Cascelloid Ltd (factory)
Camden Street (no. 3)	Fielding Sarson Ltd (leather goods manufacturer)
Rutland Street	Freeman, Hardy & Willis (shoe manufacturer)
Wimbledon Street	Faire Bros Ltd (shoe, hosiery etc. manufacturer)
Queen Street	R. Rowley (hosiery factory)
Saxby Street	dwelling house
Saville Street	dwelling house
Grove Road	dwelling house
Evington Valley Road	Crittalls Ltd (window manufacturers)
Holmfield Avenue	dwelling house
Samuel Street	LMS Goods Yards and Granary Store

Short Street East	W.H. Sharpe & Sons (builders' yard)
Guthlaxton Street	dwelling house
Eggington Street	dwelling house
Queen Street	T. Grieves & Co. (hosiery machine builders)
Severn Street	dwelling house
New Way Road	dwelling house
Kingsway Road	dwelling house
Newby Street	dwelling house
Broadway Road	dwelling house
Trueway Road	dwelling house
Kimberley Road	dwelling house
Stoughton Drive North (nos 32–4)	Palmer and Ward (motor engineers)
Temple Road	Steels & Busks (munitions factory)
The Langhill	dwelling house
Evington Valley Road	dwelling house
Evington Valley Road	dwelling house
Severn Street	gas main on fire

Appendix II

Equipment carried by Civil Defence Squads, taken from information at the Leicestershire Records Office

Anti-Gas Decontamination Squad
6 man squad (foreman and five men)
One motor vehicle for transport.
Protective oilskin suit of clothing comprising:
Jacket with hood, trousers, gloves, rubber gum boots.
Three spades.
Three picks.
Two buckets.
Two mops, or hard long-handled brushes.
Two lengths 60- to 100-ft hosepipe.
Two standpipes with adaptors.
Six 'Danger' boards.
Six Service respirators.
Two cwts of bleaching powder.
Five gallon drum of paraffin.
Seven pounds of bleach – Vaseline ointment.
Twelve pickets for enclosing contaminated areas.
Cotton waste.
Apparatus for spraying bleach onto surfaces (horticultural sprays).

ARP Clearance and Rescue Squad
6 man squad (two bricklayers, two carpenters, two plumbers, four labourers)
Standard equipment:
Two iron shod levers, 10 or 12ft long with blocks for fulcrums.
One 30cwt chain tackle (or set of rope blocks – 3 sheave and 2 sheave)
One 3-ton shackle chain.
One set sheer legs.
One single sheave snatch block.
Two hydraulic jacks with 10-ton lift.
One hydraulic jack with 20-ton lift.
One 30-ft extending ladder.
One 10-ft rope ladder.
Two portable acetylene cutting outfits with oxygen and acetylene cylinders (one-hour capacity).
One oil floodlight projector or acetylene flares.

Additional equipment
Three crowbars.
Three picks.

Three shovels.
One sledge hammer.
Two heavy axes.
Two light (timber men's) axes or mattocks.
One two-handed cross-cut saw.
Two hand saws.
One wheelbarrow.
Three 40-ft lengths 1½in Manilla lashing lines.
One 100-ft 3-in Manilla rope.
One 100-ft 4-in Manilla rope.
Three 9- × 3-in deal planks, 12-ft long.
One 100-ft wire rope.
Four electric hand lamps.
Four Hurricane Lamps.
Tarpaulins. Canvas sheets.
'Fire Devil' open fire basket for warming persons trapped.
Box of miscellaneous tools, spikes, timber dogs, etc.

Appendix III

Overview of Mobilisation and Munitions Production between September 1939 and November 1944, taken from information at the Leicestershire Records Office

(Govt White paper 'Statistics Relating to the War Effort of the United Kingdom' published 28 November 1944)

Overall output of war munitions:

102,000	aeroplanes (all types)
25,000	tanks
35,000	guns
5,700	ships

Total of national 'War Savings' campaigns:
Amount saved   £4,800,000,000

Munitions produced between September 1939 and June 1944

Naval Vessels:

Major vessels	722
Mosquito craft	1,386
Other vessels	3,636

Ground Munitions:

Tanks	25,116
Wheeled vehicles	919,111
Field artillery	13,512 (medium and heavy)
Heavy anti-aircraft	6,294
Light anti-aircraft	15,324
Machine- and sub-machine-guns	3,729,921
Rifles	2,001,949

Aircraft:

Heavy bombers	10,018
Medium and light bombers	17,702
Fighters	38,025

Women War Workers:

At the middle of 1944 out of 16 million women aged fourteen to fifty-nine, 7,100,000 were in the auxiliary services, full-time Civil Defence, or industry.

The remaining 8.9 million were mainly schoolgirls and married women with responsibilities. At the same time 900,000 were in part-time industry and 350,000 were in part-time Civil Defence.

Others were in WVS and Fire Guard.

Britain's expenditure during the five years of war has totalled £25,000,000,000 which equates to £158 10s per second.

Appendix IV

ARP Posts – Leicester City, taken from information at the *Leicestershire Mercury*

These posts were not air-raid shelters. They were places, manned by Air Raid Wardens on a 24-hour basis, at which advice on ARP matters could be sought by members of the public. Details of the location of any post in their area were circulated to householders.

'A' Division
Post no.

1, 2, 3	Store Room, St James the Greater Church, London Rd
4, 5, 6	Store Shed, Mr Morris, Avon St
7, 8, 12	ARP Office, Mill Hill Lane
13, 14	Collegiate Girls School, Lincoln St
9, 11, 15, 23	Kitchen, Methodist chapel, Clipstone St
10, 21, 22	Store Shed, Swain Street Institution (Hillcrest)
16, 18, 19	The Cottage, Thomas St
17, 24	Classroom 3, Wesley Hall, Mere Rd
20, 29, 32	Boys' Cloakroom, Charnwood St., School
25, 26, 28	Garage, Black Boy Hotel, St Saviours Rd
30	Garage, George Green, Ash St
27, 31	Beginners' Room, Newby St Congregational Church
34, 35, 36	Old Station Master's office, Great Northern station
33, 37, 38	Staff Room, Taylor St, Infant School
42, 44, 45	Caretaker's Office, Christow Street School
39, 40, 41	Garage, 172 Humberstone Rd
49, 50, 51	Scouts' Room, Methodist church, Humberstone Rd
48, 52, 54	Secular Hall, Humberstone Gate
43, 46, 47	Saddle Room, Horse Repository, Charles St
53, 55, 56	Report Centre, Rutland St

'B'Division
Post no.

1	Garage, Mr Perry, Thornton Lane
2	Staff Room, Alderman Newton Boys School, Highcross St
3	Timekeeper's Office, Adderley & Co., Market Place
4	Cell Yard, Police Cells, town hall Entrance, Bowling Green St
5	Store room, Newarke Girls School, Oxford St
6	Basement, 2 Wellington St
7	China Cellar, Victoria Hotel, Granby St
8	Stable, 'Earl Gray', Ashwell St
9	Cycle Shed, Royal Infirmary, main entrance
10, 11	Holy Trinity Day School, Regent Rd

12	Basement, 100 New Walk
13	Silent Room, Toc H, De Montfort St
14	Classroom, YMCA, Granville Rd
15	Kitchen, The Cottage, University Rd
16	Front Room, Mr Faulkner, Freemen's Common, Aylestone Rd
17	Kitchen, All Saints Church Rooms, Sawday St
18, 23, 24	Children's Room, Lifeboat Inn, New Bridge St
19	Garage, rear Bedford Hotel, Aylestone Rd
20	Room, St Andrew's Vicarage, Jarrom St
21	Garage, Crane's Haulage, Clarendon St
22	Garage, 2 Windermere St
25, 26	Skittle Alley, Westcotes Conservative Club, Wilberforce Rd
27	Cellar, 1 Westleigh Rd
28	Wash House, 140 Narborough Rd
29	Garage, Mr Refflin, Fosse Rd South
30	Garage, 49 Cambridge St
31	Stable, 107 Narborough Rd
32	Cellar, 101 Hinckley Road
33, 34	Rovers Den Room, Church of the Martyrs, Westcotes Dve
35	Ladies' Cloakroom, West End Adult School, Western Rd
36	Basement, 2 Briton St
37, 38	Stable, 35 Upperton Rd
39, 42	Store Shed, Newarke Tavern, Mill Lane
40	Report Centre, Technical School, The Newarkes
41	Store Shed, Laxton St School
43	Shed, 186 Jarrom St

'C' Division
Post no.

1	Old Station Master's Office, Great Northern station
2	Headmistress's Room, St Mark's School, Belgrave Gate
3, 5	Garage, Pineapple Inn, Archdeacon Lane
4	Friday St, depot
6	Cottage, Stead and Simpson, Mansfield St
7	Old Beer Cellar, Working Men's Club, Bond St
8	Cellar, 'Haunch of Venison', High St
9, 10	Street Cleansing Dept, Grape St, depot
11	Cellar, 2 Rayns St
12	Room, Welfare Dept, S. Russell and Sons, Bath Lane
13	Jarvis St, Depot
14	Store shed, North Bridge Inn, Frog Island
15	Garage, 15 Leamington St
16	Ladies' Room, West End Adult School, Western Rd
17	Basement, 101 Hinckley Rd
18	Skittle Alley, Dane Hill Tavern, King Richard's Rd
19	Store Shed, Tudor Hotel, Tudor Rd
20	Basement, 155 King Richard's Rd

21	Rear of Cycle Shed, Tudor Cinema, Vaughan St
22	Junior Boys' Cloakroom, Mantle Rd School
23	Cellar, 8 Central Rd
24	Kitchen, Tudor Press, Dunton St
25	Headmistress's Room, St Leonard's School, Abbey Gate
26	Abbey Hotel, Abbey Lane (Post shared with 'B' Division)

'D' Division
Post no.

1	Room at Rear Flanagan's Stores, Barkby Rd
2	Garage, 58 Kerrysdale Ave
3	Workshop, Sutton Estate Office, Gipsy Lane
4, 5	Cellar, Corporation Hotel, Catherine St, Extension
6	Room, 54 Shetland Rd
7	Girls' Locker Room, Harrison Rd School
8, 10	Garage, 195 Melton Rd
9	Office, 38 Lancashire St
11	Garage, 30 Windsor Ave
12	Garage, 130 Melton Rd
13	Cloakroom, Glen St School
14, 15	Cellar, 15 Halkin St
16	Middle Room, 4 Doncaster Rd
17, 19	Headmistress's Room, Belper St School
18	Garage, 1 Gayton Ave
20, 21	Garage, Mr Richards, Martin St
23	Gentlemen's Cloakroom, St Faith's Hall, Brandon St
22, 24	Boys' Cloakroom, Catherine St School
25	Garage, 1 Argyle St
26, 27	Wash House, Leicester Brewing and Malting Co. Ltd, Gresham St
28, 29	Timekeeper's Office, Fielding and Johnson, Ross Walk
30	Cellar, 1 Hillyard Rd
31	Shed at Rear Mr Freer, Cross St
32	Room, 2 Coral St
33, 34	Headmistress's Room, Ellis Ave School
35	Cellar, 165 Loughborough Rd
36	Cloakroom, Mellor St School
37	Kitchen, Claremont St School
38, 39	Old Saddle Room, Belgrave Hall Museum, Church Rd
40	Garage, 43 Sandringham Ave
41	Garage, 252 Abbey Lane
42, 43	229 Abbey Lane
44	Estate Office, Stocking Farm Estate
45	Ambulance Room, Hill and Cunningham, Abbey Park Rd
46	Garage, 224 Blackbird Rd
47	Cloakroom, Alderman Richard Hallam School, Anstey Lane
48	Gentlemen's Toilet Room, Speedway Hotel, Melton Rd
49, 51	Surgery, Mr Jacques, Dental Surg., Red Hill, Loughborough Rd

50	Middle Room, 66 Birstall Rd
52	Garage, 91 Curzon Ave

'E' Division
Post no.

1, 2	Garage, 38 Dovedale Rd
3	Boys' Cloakroom, Stoneleigh School, Stoneygate Rd
4	Garage, 7 Holmfield Ave
5	35 Kingsway Rd
6	Garage, 31 New Way Rd
7	Garage, 9 Trueway Rd
8	Room no. 1, St Philip's Church, Evington
9	Garage, 198 Evington Rd
10	Stock Room, 131 Evington Rd
11, 12	Cellar, Mayfield House, Mayfield Rd
13	Saddle Room, Elmfield Hotel, Elmfield Ave
14, 15	Cellar, 2a Linton St
16, 17	Lock-up Shed, Coach and Horses, Kedleston Rd
18	Cellar, 1 Eggington St
19	Old Waiting Room, 139 East Park Rd
20	Garage, 131 East Park Rd
21	Garage, 4 Kilworth Dve
22	Garage, 87 Evington Dve
23	Garage, White House, Hawthorne Dve, Evington
24	Office, Police House, Main St, Evington
25	Garage, 'Letchworth', Spencefield Lane
26, 27	Girls' Cloakroom, Moat Rd School
28	Ladies' Rest Room, Palfreyman's, Dorothy Rd
29	Gentlemen's Cloakroom, Bessant and Co., Gedding Rd
30	Stable, 214 Gwendolen Rd
31	Garage, Crown Hills Hotel
32, 33, 34	North Evington Constitutional Club, Asfordby St
35, 36	Shed, Railwaymen's Club, East Park Rd
37, 38	Girls' Cloakroom, Greenlane Rd
39, 40	Wash House, 75 Uppingham Rd
41	Infants' Cloakroom, St Barnabas School
42, 43	Skittle Alley, Working Men's Club, Frisby Rd
44	Skittle Alley, Uppingham Hotel
45, 46	Headmaster's Room, Overton Rd School
47	Garage, The Laurels Nursing Home, Uppingham Rd
48, 49	Garage, 250 Victoria Rd East
50, 52	Clay Room, Northfield House School, Gipsy Lane
51	Stable, 4 Ireton Rd
53, 54	Garage, 326 Humberstone Lane, Thurmaston
55	Waiting Room, Lodge gates, City Mental Hospital
56	Medical Room, Mundella School, Overton Rd
57	Room 68, Pine Tree Ave

58	Garage, 96 Scraptoft Lane
59	Kitchen, 41 Wigley Rd
60, 61	Coach House, Manor House, Humberstone
62	Store Room, 83 Clumber Rd
63	Store Room, Coleman Rd Jnr School
64, 65	Store Shed, Full Moon Hotel, Coleman Rd
66	Garage, 261 Uppingham Rd
67	Garage, 327 Uppingham Rd
68	Garage, 25 Westmeath Ave
69	Garage, 236 Scraptoft Lane
70	Garage, 61 Havencrest Dve

'F' Division
Post no.

1, 2	Weir's Garage, Fleetwood Rd
3,6	Cellar of Knighton Fields House Domestic Science College, Welford Rd
4	Shower Room, Sir Jonathan North School, Knighton Lane
5	Caretaker's Quarters, Avenue Rd School
7, 10	Conservative Club, Queen's Rd
8, 9	Garage, 112a Howard Rd
11	Garage, rear Lyndhurst School, Knighton Park Rd
12	Stable at 1 Central Ave
13	Rear Room, Rangers Club Room, Chapel Lane
14	Booking Office, Kenwood swimming pool, Knighton Church Rd West
15, 16	Dressing Room, University playing fields, Welford Rd
17	Garage, 1 Stoneygate Ave
18	Saddle Room, 15 Elms Rd
19, 20	Gentlemen's Cloakroom, Holbrook Rd Memorial Hall
21	Garage, 51 Ring Rd
22	Office, Gasworks, Aylestone Rd
23, 26	Adult School, Knighton Lane
24	282 Aylestone Rd
25	Middle Cloakroom, Knighton Fields School
27	Garage, 341 Saffron Lane
28	9 Cyprus Rd
29, 30	Annexe to Metal Room, Linwood Lane School
31	Headmistress's Room, Marriott Rd School
32, 33	Store Room, Park Estate Library, Saffron Lane
34	Registrar's Office, Saffron Hill cemetery, Stonesby Ave
35	101 Wigston Lane
36	Garage, 6 Monsell Drive
37, 38	Infants' Changing Room, Granby Rd Schools
39	Gentlemen's Room, Church Rooms, Church Rd

'G' Division
Post no.

1	Garage, Blackbird Hotel, Blackbird Rd
2	Archdeacon Lane Memorial Hall, Buckminster Rd
3	Cellar, Mr Harris, Petrol Station, Groby Rd
4, 5	Wash House, Empire Hotel, Fosse Rd North
6	Cellar, St Augustine's Vicarage, Pool Rd
8	Infants' Nursery Cloakroom, Ingle St School
9, 12	Stable, Mr Gimson, Gimson Rd Corner, Glenfield Rd
10	Room 1, Wentworth Rd
11, 13	Kitchen, St Paul's School, Kirby Rd
14	Garage, 247 Hinckley Rd
15	Garage, 21 Meadhurst Rd
16	Garage, 16 Westfield Rd
17	Garage, 34 Hilder's Rd
18	Garage, Corner House, Western Park Rd and Hinckley Rd
19	Kitchen, Westcotes Congregational Church, Hinckley Rd
20, 47	Hinckley Rd School
21, 22	Cellar, 15 Redmarle Rd
23	Room Adjoining Shower Baths, Hamlin Rd School
24	Teachers' Room, Cort Crescent School
25	Cellar, Shoulder of Mutton Hotel, Heyford Rd
26	Storeroom, Benbow Rise School
27	Garage, Densham Chemists, Raven Rd
28	Basement, 126 Westcotes Dve
29	Garage, corner Upperton Rd and Fosse Rd South
30, 31	Stable, 4 Compton Rd
32	Tool Shed, Haddenham Rd School
33	Room, 23 Lavender Rd
34	Garage, corner Chartley Rd and Winchester Ave
35	Garage, 62 Imperial Ave
36	Room, 88 Newfields Ave
37	Medical Room, Caldecote Rd School
38	Room, 8 Bainbridge Rd
39	Outhouse, Custance Farm, Rowley Fields Ave
40	Garage, 1 Meredith Rd
41	Garage, 47 Somerville Rd
42	Garage, 94 Evesham Rd
43	Wooden Shed, Ellesmere Rd School
44	Staff Cloakroom, Folville Rise School
45	Room, 10 Winton Ave
46	Room, 28 Mountcastle Rd
48	Garage, 115 Dorchester Rd

Glossary

ADO	Assistant Divisional Officer (Fire Services)
AFS	Auxiliary Fire Service
ARP	Air Raid Precautions
ATS	Auxiliary Territorial Service
DO	Divisional Officer (Fire Services)
DUKW	General Motors amphibious landing craft
FANY	First Aid Nursing Yeomanry
HE	High Explosive
HMF	His Majesty's Forces
IRA	Irish Republican Army
LMS	London Midland & Scottish Railway
LNER	London & North Eastern Railway
Luftwaffe	German Air Force
NAAFI	Navy, Army, Air Force Institute
NCO	non-commissioned officer
NFS	National Fire Service
OCTU	Officer Cadet Training Unit
PAMS	Police Auxiliary Messenger Service
PoW	Prisoner of War
RAF	Royal Air Force
ROC	Royal Observer Corps
SC	Special Constable
USAAF	United States Army Air Force
VES	Voluntary Emergency Service
WAAF	Women's Auxiliary Air Force
WRNS	Women's Royal Naval Service
WVS	Women's Voluntary Service

Bibliography

Armed Forces of World War II, The, Andrew Mollo, Orbis Publishing, 1981

Aviation in Leicestershire, Roy Bonser, Midland Publishing, 2001

Bird's Eye Wartime Leicester, Terence C. Cartwright, TCC Publications, 1998

Bombers Over Berlin, Alan W. Cooper, Patrick Stephens Ltd, 1985

British Army Uniforms & Insignia of World War Two, Brian L. Davis, Arms and Armour Press, 1983

Daily Telegraph Record of the Second World War, The, *Daily Telegraph*, Sidgwick & Jackson/*Daily Telegraph*, 1989

Dictionary of World War II, Ian Hogg, Hutchinson, 1994

Fire Service Memories, Aylmer Firebrace, Sir, Andrew Melrose

History of the German Air Force, Bryan Philpott, Gallery Books, 1986

History of the Royal Air Force, Michael Sharpe, Parragon Books, 2002

History of World War I, A.J.P. Taylor, MacDonald & Co., 1988

Home Guard, The, S.P. Mackenzie, Oxford University Press, 1995

Leicester's Battle Against Fire, Malcolm Tovey, Anderson Publications, 1982

Leicester in the Twentieth Century, David Nash & David Reeder, Sutton Publishing, 1993

Leicester in the Fifties, Steve England, Douglas Goodlad, and Anita Syvret, Archive Publications/*Leicester Mercury*, 1989

Leicester Past and Present, Jack Simmons, Eyre Methuen, 1974

Magnificent Mercury, Steve England, Kairos Press, 1999

Municipal Journal, Leics City Council, September 1956

Post-War Kitchen, Margueritte Patten, Hamlyn, 1998

Royal Air Force Cosford. The War Years, A.E. Joyner, RPC Cosford, 1994

Royal Leicestershire Regiment 17th Foot, The, W.E Underhill (Brigadier), Antony Rowe

SS: Hitler's Instrument of Terror, The, Gordon Williamson, Book Club Associates, 1994

Third Reich at War, Michael Veranov, Sienna, 1998

Tigers, The, J.M.K. Spurling, Leicester Museums, 1969

Transport Memories of Leicestershire, Peter Hollins, Manor Publications/*Leicester Mercury*, 1990

When the War Came to Leicester, G.H. Ingles, Pamphlet

Women at War 1939–1945, The Home Front, Carol Harris, Sutton Publishing, 2000

Women in Wartime, Jane Waller & Michael Vaughan-Rees, Optima, 1987

Index

Acquisition of Food (Excessive Quantities) Order 1939 87
Acton, Frank 14, 46, 108
Air Raid Precautions Act 1937 8
Ambulance Service 79
American Forces Club 100
Anderson, C.A. 137
Anderson, Sir John 28
Anstee, S. 108
Anti-Aircraft Battery 45
Armer, Peggy 56
Arnold, PC 159
ARP Controller 8, 25, 28, 33, 35, 74, 133, 149, 171
Atkins, A.H. 39
Auld, James 96
Auxiliary Fire Service (AFS) 32, 47, 74, 80, 91, 137, 157

Bailey, Frederick 158
Ball, Jack 55
Barrett, J.C. (VC) 18
Beaverbrook, Lord 50
Beckett, John L. 161–5, 171, 175
Bennett, Leonard Percival 159
Beveridge, Sir William 102, 125, 141
Bevin, Ernest 75–6, 123, 142
Bird, Lily 158
Bosworth, E.H. 146
Bowden, Herbert 169
British Red Cross Society 81, 86, 100, 105, 128–9
Broadhurst, Walter 8
Browett's 59
Brown, M. 108
Browne, G.F., First Aid Commandant 30
Burnham Committee 46, 155
Burrows, David 50
Burton, Richard Henry 158
Buxton, Clifford 86
Buxton, Frank 86
Buxton, George Edward 96, 97

Callander, C.B. 41
Cant, Albert 86
Capital 'T' Club 100
Chamberlain, Neville 5, 18, 20, 41

Chief Fire Officer 7
Chief Labour Supply Officer 142
Churchill, Winston 18, 41, 42, 150, 165, 169
Civil Defence Duties (Compulsory Enrolment) Order 1941 74
Cleansing and Waste Department 48, 88
Cleaver, Roland 86, 96
Clewlow, Alfred 97
Cole, Oswald John Buxton, Chief Constable 7, 8, 12, 26, 28, 35, 37, 83, 95, 150, 159
Control of Noise Order 165
Cort, Lord Mayor, Councillor 81
Cowle, William Alfred 130–1
Cramp, Arthur 81, 93, 137
Croft, Lord 42
Cromwell, Lord 23, 105

Daniell, George 86
Defence Regulations 1939 32
Denman, Lady 144
Dickens, George 55
Dilks, Alan 131
Director of Education 72, 155
Dog Stadium 96, 175
Donovan, Terence Norbert 169
Doran, Kenneth, Christopher 19
Dowager Marchioness of Reading 139
Draycott, Doria Lilian 96

Eden, Anthony 42, 103
Edge, William 169
Education Act 123, 155–6
Electricity Department 22, 105
Emergency Committee 14, 31, 74
Emergency Powers and Defence Regulations 108
Essential Works Order 79
Evans, William 85
Everard, Sir W. Lindsay 169

Faire Brothers 59
Farmer, J.W. 55
Field Regiment, Royal Artillery 18
Finlinson, John 14, 108
Fire Brigade Act 1937 32
Fire Brigade 8, 23, 28, 35, 65, 70, 79–81, 173

Fire Prevention (Business Premises) Order 1941 70
Fire Services Act 1947 173
Fire Watchers Order 1940 32
First Police Reserve 10
Food Control Committee 14, 48, 106, 108–9, 116, 121
Food Shop Workers Charter 115
Food (Restrictions of Meals in Establishments) Order 114
Foot, Robert 152
Fouquies, Capt 95
Frears, John 23
Freeman, Hardy & Willis 59
Fry, Elizabeth 95
Fuel Office – Overseer 120, 123, 152
Fyfe, James 31

Gabbitas, John 12
Garrett, E.B. 65
Gas Department 8
General Defence Regulations 146
German, Guy 17, 39
Gillot, Charles 23
Girls Training Corps 123
Goddard, Reg Sgt-Maj 90
Gooseman, Arthur 161
Greasley, John 108
Grieves' factory 60
Gwynne-Vaughan, Helen 139

Hadfield's chemistsshop 60
Hadley, Cyril 150
Hannah, John V.C. 102
Harris, A.J. 65
Hart & Levy 59
Hastings, Dr Somerville 134
Hawkes, Brian 64
Hazelrigg, Sir Arthur 89
Henderson, Sir Nevile Meyrick 5
Hendry, A. 108
Higgott, John 64
HMS Renown 88, 130, 132
Hodgkinson, Albert 132
Home Guard 42-4, 68, 76, 85, 89–90, 95, 103–4, 130, 137, 145, 156
Hore-Belisha, Leslie 126
Hosiery Union 47
Huddard 159

Jackson, Elizabeth 132
Jackson, F.T. 108
Jacobs, Sady 158
James Hearth & Co. 60
James Lulham & Co. 60
Janner, Barnett 169

Johnson, Albert 96
Johnson, Frederick Arthur 85
Jones, Eileen Louvaine 96–7

Keene, Charles 14, 23, 30, 35, 50, 74, 126, 171
Kemp's Ltd 59
Kenshall, SC 159
Kerrison, Oscar 28
Kimball, Lawrence 169

Labour Advisory Committee 142
Laffin, A. 108
Lasky, Mr 62
Lee, L. 65
Leicester City Football Club 58, 93, 95
Leicester City Police 23, 65, 150, 159
Leicester Co-operative Society 53, 66, 75, 101, 108, 119
Leicester Mercury 48, 55, 78–9, 81, 102, 105, 107, 142, 165
Leicester War Emergency Committee 42
Leicestershire Regiment 17, 41–2, 45, 53, 81, 90, 94, 130, 175
Liddell, Gen Sir Clive 130
Lighting Department 152, 166
Lincoln, James 90
Llewellin, J.J. 116, 121
Local Defence Volunteers (LDV) 42–3, 90, 103
Lowry, J.H. 142
Lyons, Abraham Montagu 169

MacPherson, Andrew 19
Magnay, Harold 72
Mann, Lawrence 131–2
Mark, Robert 150
Marsh, Ivy 64–5
Marshall, George C. 121
McEvoy, Lawrence 14, 108
McKinnell, Errington 35, 81, 173
Military Service Act 47
Mining Association 152
Ministry of Food 73, 105, 109–10, 112, 114, 126
Ministry of Fuel and Power 152
Ministry of Health 37, 134
Ministry of Home Security 165
Ministry of Labour and National Service 144
Ministry of Reconstruction 126
Ministry of Supply 77, 153
Minto, John 156, 165
Minty, William 119
Moffatt, Jack 104–5
Moon, A.A. 105
Moore Eady Murcott & Goode 59
Morland, Florence 146

Morrison, Herbert 33, 73, 77, 94, 149
Mott, Eliza 69
Mould John 22
Muddimer, Ernest 87

National Defence Corps 90
National Fire Service (NFS) 35, 79, 81, 91, 93–4, 126, 137, 147, 149, 173
National Joint Industrial Council 102
National Milk Scheme 113
National Service & Armed Forces Act 1939 73, 76
National Service Hostels Association 148
National Work Notice 146
Neal 90
Neighbours Leagues 47, 48
Netherwood, Arthur 81
Newberry, Gordon Arthur 97

Olorenshaw, H.C. 108
Orton, Eric 132
Overseas Reception Board 49

PoW Relatives Association 86
Parbury, George 50, 108
Paterson, William 28
Patrick, T.H. 135
Patriotic Fund 50, 100
Payne, Nora Emily 130–2
Pentney, James 151
Petit, Gen 81
Pickering, Ernest Harold 169
Piggott, J.I. 156
Police and Firemen (War Service) Act 1939 32
Police Auxilliary Messenger Service 7, 133
Police War Reserve 10, 25, 47, 73
Poole, Harold 8
Portal 126–7, 154
Preston, T. 108
Prisoners of War Comforts Fund 82, 127–8
Pulford, Charles 55

Quisling, Vikdun 39

RAF Expansion Plan 19
Reconstruction Committee 126
Regional ARP Commissioner 23
Registration of Employment Act 142
Reinstatement Officer 157
Reith, Lord 74
Rescue, Shoring and Demolition Section 31, 41
Ritter, Maxwell 35
Road, Sewers and Repairs Parties 41
Roberts, Thomas Bruce 137
Rooney, Frederick 18
Roosevelt, Franklin Delano 18

Rudkin, Florence 132
Rumsey, L.E. 21
Rushcliffe, Lord 148
Russell, Percy 102

'Salute the Soldier Week' 130
Sandys, Duncan 134
Schools Medical Service 49
Sharman, H.T. 108
Shephard. S. 70
Sherriff, Amos 106
Simon, Sir John 22, 37, 108
Simpson, Mrs (WVS) 140
Smith, Tacker 96
Special Constabulary 12, 35, 95, 137, 166
Spitfire Fund 50, 86
St John's Ambulance Service 7, 30, 32, 65, 95, 100
Steels and Busks 66
Stewart, Agnes, Mother Gonzague de Marie 128–9
Stokes, D.R. 119
Swainson, Cllr Mrs 108
Swann, Sir Oliver 81
Sykes, Frank 96, 175

T. Simpson & Co. 119
T. Venables Ltd 60
Tams, Leslie 105
Territorial Army 45
Thiele, Claud 100
Thorpe, Nellie 85
Thorpe, Thomas William 85
Tigers Rugby Football Club 59
Training and National Service Act 39
Tramways Department 42
Transport Department 85–6, 101, 107, 148, 150-1, 164
Tree, Ronald 169
Trent, Lord 23
Tyler, H.W.H. 89
Tyrwhitt, Sir Reginald 88

United Nations Day 95
United Services Club 100

'V Sign Club' 148
Venn, Charles 13
Vice Printing Works, Calais Hill 59
Voluntary Emergency Service (VES) 18

Wakeling, Albert 158
Warren, Arnold 85
Warren, John William 159
'Warship Week' 88
Water Department 152

Waterhouse, Charles 169
Wells, C. 65
Weston, J. 65
White, William 82
Wilford, Alderman 80
Wilkinson, Roland 87
Wilson, Hugh 48
Winteringham, Francis 7–8, 10, 25–6, 32, 35
Women's Auxiliary Police Corps 12
Women's Services Club 100

Women's Voluntary Service (WVS) 7, 32, 48, 95,
    123, 133–4, 138–40, 142, 153
Wood, A.E. 41
Wood, Sir Kingsley 91, 98
Woods, PC John 131
Woolton, Lord 111, 114, 116, 126
Worthington, Charles 72, 74, 133, 149, 171, 173
Wykes, Alfred Lancelot 130

Young Soldiers Battalion 90